"BACK IN THE DAY!"

"Back In the Day!"

A Journey to Success

The Autobiography & Writings of

Betty Carolyn Isaac McDaniel

XULON PRESS

Xulon Press
2301 Lucien Way #415
Maitland, FL 32751
407.339.4217
www.xulonpress.com

Unless otherwise indicated, Scripture quotations taken from the King James Version (KJV) – *public domain.*

Printed in the United States of America.

Paperback ISBN-13: 978-1-6322-1877-3
eBook ISBN-13: 978-1-6322-1878-0

INTRODUCTION

I started out writing what was supposedly to be my Obituary; but as I continued to write, I realized I had a lot to say, and it would take up more than one page. Therefore, I ask you to journey along with me as I reminisce about my life and the years that the Lord blessed me with, along with a wonderful family and wonderful experiences. It was filled with good times, bad times, and all kinds of times in between. I learned a lot. I grew a lot. It is my hope that this book will enlighten and enrich you too.

Betty Carolyn Isaac McDaniel, Author

DEDICATION

This book is dedicated to my children: Linda, Paul, and Maria; and to my grandchildren:

Aliyah; Valdon, III; Ananda; Imani; and Jarrel. May they learn about our past, look ahead to the future and apply some of the golden gems presented throughout this work.

Also, to my siblings: Irma, Doris, Homer, Jr., and Brenda; may they read the book with much interest and joy, since they are very much a part of the story too.

And lastly, to anyone seeking the truth, and wants to learn how to successfully apply The Word of God to their own lives, so that they too can walk victoriously into their own destiny.

ACKNOWLEDGEMENTS

I would first of all like to thank my Lord and Savior, Jesus Christ, for putting on my heart the thoughts and desires to write this Biography. It appeared to be a monumental task, but as I listened to the Holy Spirit, and followed His lead, it became more doable and a labor of love. His promptings and bringing things back to memory, encouraged me to see the job through, and understand that a lot of people would be blessed by my experiences. I yielded, and began the journey of sharing, encouraging and enlightening others.

Also, a special thanks to my daughter, Linda, who, without her untiring help, this book would not have been published. Her computer skills, time, and patience, kept me focused and moving ahead, despite the many setbacks and road-blocks. Her labor of love and encouragement will always have a warm place in my heart. For this I thank her sincerely.

My husband, Walter, was also a source of knowledge and help: proof reading texts, helping to weed out non-essential information, supplying ink and paper, sending my writings to be stored in 'the cloud', and other technical procedures that I knew nothing about! For this I profusely thank him too.

And to you, the reader, may you be blessed, encouraged, and informed; and may this biography change your life for-ever, for the good.

TABLE OF CONTENTS

Chapter 1

THE BEGINNING

I was born on January 22, 1938, in Oklahoma City, Oklahoma, to the parents of Homer Lee Isaac, and Bettie Mary Douglas. I was named after my Mother and Great Grandmother. The family always called me 'Carolyn', to differentiate between the Bettys. (I also had two cousins named Betty.) I was in my 70's before I learned that my mother was Native American, (Choctaw and Cherokee), which made me 50% Native American and 50% African American (DNA confirmed). I found this very interesting, since as kids, when we went home to Oklahoma to visit, from Phila., our friends would ask us when we got back if we saw any Indians. If I had known then, I would have told them, "You're looking at one!" (Especially my mother!)

America had us hoodwinked in that they said if you had one drop of Negro blood in you, or had one ounce of color, then you were black. My mother and siblings were fair skinned, and my father and I were brown skinned. They say I looked just like him, or as one of his friends said, "You spit that one out!"; so, I had no idea that I was partially Native American. The old folks didn't talk about those things, back in the day.

I enjoyed telling people that I was born in Oklahoma. Most of my friends and people I knew came from down south. Eyebrows would go up when I said I was born in Oklahoma. Later on I figured it out; it was part of my personality that I loved to be different or stand out from the crowd.

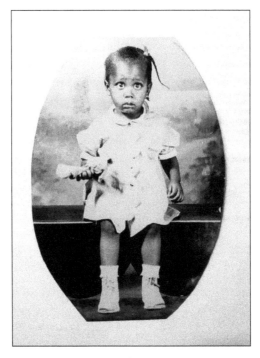

Betty Carolyn at Age 2

My parents moved to Philadelphia from Oklahoma when I was 2 years old. We stayed with Dad's older brother, Vernon Isaac, for a short time, and then we moved into an apartment on South Street, around 19th. Later we found a permanent home at 1309 S. Napa St., still in South Philly. My older sisters, Irma, and Doris, and I, were all born in Oklahoma. My brother, Homer Lee Isaac, Jr., and my baby sister, Brenda, were born in Philadelphia. My mother didn't believe in giving birth in hospitals (they might mix up her babies, she said), so I woke up one morning to loud wails and crying from a baby in her bedroom. All I knew was that I was no longer the baby; and had been replaced by a brother. Bummer!

The Oklahoma Siblings:
Betty Carolyn, Doris Marie & Irma Jean

Talk about replacement! It doesn't stop there. I was away at college and casually called home and asked my sisters what was new. They said, "Mother is pregnant!" (I later found out it was a girl!) I couldn't even claim to be the baby girl anymore; I was a middle child! Too late. I was grown by then. I could at least still say I was <u>raised</u> the baby girl!

What was life like, growing up in the 1940's and 1950's in South Philadelphia? We lived on a very, small street, 'Napa', between 31st and 32nd Streets, between Wharton and Reed Streets, better known as the Grays Ferry section of Philadelphia. Our street was so small that you could jump across it in 2 or 3 leaps. (We tried it.) You could only drive one way, so my dad had to park partially on the sidewalk so other cars could get by.

They were all row houses with two rooms and a kitchen downstairs, and two rooms and a bathroom upstairs. I often wondered how large families with 6-8 children made out (and there were some). My parents added an addition to our house that gave us a 3rd bedroom. We were buying our house, as opposed to most others who were renting, or just needing temporary housing, or it was simply all they could afford. As children, we didn't care. All we wanted to do was play and have fun.

Our street was our playground, and boy, did we use it. We drew hopscotch on the ground, drew bases for baseball, drew squares for King Fish, played Babies in the Air, Red Light, Jump rope, etc. You name it and we played it. The back of the Movie Theater was on our side of the street, with alleys on either side. Sometimes we would match up and have races around the theater to see who could run the fastest. The fellows used to make scooters out of our old skates, a crate from the produce store, and an old board. They would ride us up and down the street in the crate part. Some of my playmates were: Jeanette and Loretta; Robert and Julius; Della and Eugene; and many others; but these were the ones who were around my age.

Our street was also our 'social media', and that's where we learned what was going on; who was going with whom, what was the latest gossip, where was the next event, who was pregnant, who hit the numbers, who got locked up, etc., etc. We had phones, but they were rotary, and some people had a party line, which meant you shared it with other people and could only talk on it at certain times. If you didn't have a phone, people called you on the corner store's phone, and someone had to go and get you. They would give you a nickel or a dime for coming to get them.

One of our favorite activities during the summer was playing in the fire hydrant. The fellows would turn the fire hydrant on, and we would splash each other and have a grand old time. Someone would call the cops and we would all have to run and scatter home while they turned it off and left. When they did, we would do it again until they got tired of coming.

Sometimes we would make popsicles, by placing Kool-Aid in our ice trays, and selling them to neighborhood kids for one or two cents. That was our first try at being in business and learning to make money. Actually, our dad, did briefly open up a small restaurant in our basement, behind our mother's beauty shop. He sold home-made pies and cakes and sandwiches. Mother couldn't run the shop, bake, and cook the food too, take care of her family, do hair, and a multiplicity of other things, so that adventure was short lived.

We used to receive bottled milk on our doorstep, and salesmen would come around in horse and buggies selling fish, meats, and vegetables. The insurance man would come around, once a month or so, and allow you to pay a small amount on a policy; usually under $1.00.

When someone died, the body was brought to the home for a few days, to allow the neighbors to come over and see, visit, and comfort the family.

Dad found a piano teacher for us when I was about 7 or 8. His name was Professor Randolph, and he always wore a suit and carried a black satchel. You can imagine how this went down with the neighborhood kids. We got teased a lot.

My Dad was also famous for home spun philosophies or lessons. In addition to telling us that we could do anything anyone else could do because we had two hands, two eyes, two feet, etc., he also told us that we should do what successful people do. If they lean to the right, then you lean to the right (he would lean to show us). If they lean to the left, you lean to the left. If they lean forward, you lean forward. I guess he was trying to explain to us that we should emulate successful people. I really didn't understand it all at the time, as a kid; I just thought that Dad was funny!

THE FAMILY

Back Row: Irma, Doris, Chuck, Betty Carolyn
Front Row: Homer, Brenda & Bettie Mary

Many times, he would share about his own childhood experiences back in Oklahoma; like the time he rallied his whole class up, and they all went down to the principal's office to complain about a teacher. Or the time he got shot in the leg on the school bus after having an altercation with another student. (He'd show us the scar.) Or, on a more positive note, how he was especially proud of the fact that he was the youngest student ever to play with the high school band while still in grade school. He played the saxophone, (evidently very well), and joined them in playing at the State Fair.

Another characteristic of Dad was that he believed in telling us the truth or the bare facts.

He would tell us 'so and so' stabbed somebody, or someone was locked up for some offence, or someone had a family outside of their marriage, etc. Mother was horrified and told him he shouldn't tell us such things; but should let us enjoy our childhood. We had to learn to balance the horrific things in life with everyday events. It didn't come easy; and it took a while.

I remember one day when Mother was upstairs in bed sick, when a bill collector came calling. Back in the day, if you fell behind in your bills, they would send someone out to your house and try to embarrass you in front of your neighbors, as they called you out, outside of your door, about being delinquent. My sister, Doris, answered the door and then went upstairs to tell Mother who it was. She said to tell them, 'She wasn't home'. When Doris gave the man the message, he began to rant and rave, and said, "I know your mother is here. I heard her. Mrs. Isaac, why don't you pay your bills, and I wouldn't have to come around and hound you about payments, etc., etc., etc.

Mother crawled out of the bed, wobbled down the stairs holding shakily onto the handrail, confronted the man at the door, and said, "When I say I'm not at home...I'm not at home!" and slammed the door in his face; then struggled back upstairs to her sick bed. I understand a red-faced collector slunk away.

You have to remember that, during this time, we lived under America's mandate that, blacks were: Last to be hired, first to be fired, and paid less than everybody else. We were also given more of the menial jobs. It was hard finding and keeping work, let alone making a decent salary to take care of your family. But we pressed on, trusting in God to turn things around.

Mother and dad had a complicated relationship. As kids, we didn't understand all of their ups and downs in a marital situation. What we did learn was that all marriages have challenges, and good and bad times, and that couples have to learn how to work things out. They stayed together for over 50 years; I think they learned how it goes.

Later on in life, when Walter and I went into the ministry, and had to counsel young couples, one of the things we shared with them was that marriage was not always a fifty/fifty deal. Sometimes it was a ninety/ten deal, and not in your favor! You would have to learn how to compromise, sometimes put the other person first, and above all, you must have a way of communicating and sharing and vocalizing your thoughts. You must listen to one another and be willing to change. (Read: Eph. 4:29-32). We summed it up with the 3-C's: Christ, first; Communication, second; and Compromise, third. And lastly, we told them to keep their marriage alive. We always celebrated birthdays, holidays, and special events. Valentine's Day always came with a card and a box of candy, sometimes with flowers.

The other thing we did, like clockwork, was to have a weekly Friday night, "Date Night".

It always started with dinner out, sometimes followed by a movie or a show. This gave us personal time together; and allowed us to catch up on what was going on with each other.

Chapter 2

OUR NEIGHBORHOOD

There was an icehouse on one end of our street, and a chicken house and grocery store on the other end. You would pick out the chicken that you wanted, and the owner would ring its neck for you, take off the feathers, cut it up, and then you would take it home to Momma. I was the youngest of three girls, so I didn't have to go through that ordeal. My oldest sister, Irma, took care of that! Sometimes my next to the oldest sister, Doris, did the honors too.

Irma and Doris had to drag a large block of ice from the ice store to put in the ice box at home. There was no refrigerator. We also had to wash clothes on a scrub board; there was no washer and dryer. Clothes were hung outside on a clothesline. Mom and Dad did the best they could, but money was scarce, and jobs paid little. They had fairly good jobs, during the war, (World War II), and afterwards, Mother decided to go to Apex Cosmetology School, where she got her credentials and began doing hair in the home. I think it was $1.00 or $2.00 for a press and curl. They eventually remodeled the basement into a Beauty Shop, now Mom could work from home and keep up with 3 busy kids, at that time.

We had lots of neighborhood stores: barber shop, drugstore, shoe store, bakery, butcher, etc. It was a thriving community, but there were glaring disparities. For example, the blacks lived on 5 or 6 small streets, and the whites lived in larger surrounding homes with porches and more rooms. Yes, life was unfair, but we had to learn to deal with it. Another example was, we had no playground, but the white community did. We tried to play over there, but they would throw rocks at us, or sic their dogs on us, and we would run home. Did I mention the name calling?

Although we lived next door to a movie, we were not allowed in. When they finally let us in, we had to sit in the balcony or to the side. It eventually evolved, but I'm talking about back in my day. When we went into town, we weren't allowed to try on hats or clothing. Store owners watched us closely and followed us around like hawks. They would skip waiting on us sometimes, and move on to white customers, serving us last, if at all!

Speaking of name calling, my dad at one time, drove a city trolley. One day a white man got off the trolley and called him the "N" word. Dad stopped the trolley in the middle of the street, grabbed an iron crowbar, and took off running after him. (Thank God he didn't catch him.) Yes, prejudice will do that to you. It takes years of forgiveness and growing in your faith to get these images out of your head, and to learn not to hate. Later on, as black and white relations evolved, Dad had a white lawyer friend who always gave him tickets to major games: football, baseball, boxing, etc., so times do change. Dad came a long way from chasing a white man down the street, to having strong connections with people regardless of their race, or color.

Dad worked at a number of jobs to keep food on the table. In addition to driving a trolley, he later drove a cab, worked as a shipping clerk, and ran a parking lot for years near Broad and South Street in Phila. Ultimately, he retired from the Philadelphia School Board, having worked as the 'Lead non-Teaching Assistant' at Bok High School. Dad was funny. He said he was going to retire at 62 on his exact birthday (April 17), and so he did! This was a man who meant what he said, literally!

Speaking of April 17, years later when I was pregnant with my son, Paul, his due date was April 16. My dad asked me if I could wait one more day, and have him on the 17th, his birthday. Ha, ha; very funny! Paul arrived on time and on his exact due date, April 16!

Mother was an excellent seamstress, and sewed uniforms for the military during World War II. She too, eventually worked for, and retired from the Phila. School Board, as a 'Home and School Coordinator'.

Baseball! Dad was quite an athlete. He played semi-pro ball, and always wanted lots of boys to fuel his passion. We always said that the Lord has a sense of humor. What did He give my dad, you might ask? Three girls, right in a row. Dad was done! About 7 or 8 years later, Jackie Robinson came on the scene, the first black to play on a major league baseball team. Dad said he'd give it one more shot. Yippie! It's a boy! But here's the kicker; my brother took after my mother's side of the family, who were low key and laid back, and nowhere near as aggressive as my dad's people. Did my brother even like sports? Oh, yes, I think it was Soccer!

Dad started a girls' softball team and I was the pitcher. I was very athletic and competitive and a tomboy. I guess my dad said he'd work with what he had. I would climb trees, climb roofs, play aggressive competitive games, etc. Life was great!

Second Row, third from left, Betty Carolyn

Our neighborhood, or more specifically, our street, was like a family. Any adult neighbor could correct you or let you know that they'd report you to your parents if you misbehaved. And they did! Back in the day, spankings and whippings were commonplace, so you hated it when a neighbor reported you. We also hated to hear my mother say, "Wait until your father gets home!" We knew there was going to be a beating for sure, even if your mother spanked you on the spot beforehand.

Let's talk about corporal punishment and child abuse. To me, if you get physically corrected for doing wrong, end of story, as long as it's reasonable and appropriate for the offense. Child abuse comes under the category of someone physically or verbally abusing you for no other reason other than they can, or that they had a bad day, or that you were an inconvenience, or that they had some emotional issues. Read your bible. It tells you all about sparing the rod and how it will bring grief to your parents and trouble to your soul. (In the Book of Proverbs). More on this later.

I won't say we were poor, poor, but money was scarce. If my mother bought us a blouse a piece, we had to interchange and share with our sisters, thus you would have 3 blouses instead of one. If shoe soles developed holes, you had to stuff them with newspaper or cardboard until you could get another pair. I think we even tried gluing or pinning them at one time.

My dad had a friend, Mr. Green, who worked for a rich white family. They would always give him their cast-off clothing; and since he didn't have any kids of his own, he would give the bags of clothing to my dad for us. We would rummage through those bags like they were gifts from heaven. We often found some really nice items, that expanded our wardrobe as if we had gone shopping at Macy's. Sometimes, it's the little things in life.

On holidays, especially Christmas, there was no such thing as a bike a piece...one for all! Take turns. Since we were the only ones on the street with a bike, we would allow the other kids to take a ride to the corner and back. I remember one of the boys asked to ride, and he didn't come back until dark! That was the end of that!

My mom was very thrifty. Remember, they had just come out of the Great Depression, so they knew about hard times. My mother refused to take welfare or government handouts. She would rather scrub floors or do housework. I guess they were too proud or thought that everyone should carry their own weight.

I remember when we were little, Mother used to pull us around (3 girls), in a little red wagon and took us to work with her while she cleaned houses. A babysitter was out of the question. That would eat up all of her money. We didn't understand all of the dynamics here, we just thought it was fun, and enjoyed playing outside until she finished. At any event, I believe my parents did the best they could with what they had. God bless them both.

Since we didn't have much money, my parents looked for inexpensive activities to keep us busy or entertained. Some days, usually after church, they would drive us to the airport to watch the planes take off. Sometimes they would take us to Father Devine's Restaurant to get a good meal. (All you had to do was to leave a small donation.) On hot summer days, they would take us to the free city pool, League Island, for a cooling splash; or sometimes we kids would walk to the museum to see the mummies.

One of my favorite outings was driving through North Philly and watching all the action there. If you thought South Philly was something, try North Philly! We would conclude the outing by visiting our cousins, (Dad's brother, Lincoln

Isaac's children.) He had 7 or 8 kids and we always enjoyed playing with them, especially with the oldest, Betty Jo, who was closer to our age. We also had cousins near us in South Philly: Ricky, Connie, Michael, Susan and Eugene, Jr., but they were younger. (Children of Dad's younger brother, Eugene Isaac.)

When we became teenagers, girls began to get pregnant and boys began to disappear. Some went into the military, and some went to jail. I wanted none of this, and I was determined there would be no babies. I had bigger plans. And besides, I really didn't see any neighborhood boys that interested me romantically. I didn't even know what romance really was, other than what I had read in books and novels, or what I had seen in the movies.

Another thing that bothered me was how some of the neighborhood women dressed. They wore shapeless, faded dresses, and creeled over shoes and their hair was a wreck. I made up my mind, then and there, that when I got older, even if I gained weight, I would keep my hair groomed and my clothes 'correct'. Even to this day, I will not leave the house without tending to my appearance. Later on, I learned that I had the gift of "Discernment", (Heb. 5:14), the ability to tell right from wrong, or, how to tell what works and what doesn't. Whereas some people would complain—I didn't have this; momma didn't do that; daddy wasn't there; I lived in a ghetto, etc., etc. My whole thing was, I'm not going out like that. I'm not letting that happen in my life. In other words, things that didn't seem right, I wanted just the opposite. I didn't know it was a gift; I thought everybody could figure that out!

Another discernment I had, and figured out later on in life was, that two paychecks were better than one. I have always worked. I guess I just wanted better. The Lord provided me with teaching jobs wherever we lived. Whether it was in Pennsylvania, New Jersey, California, North Carolina, or Missouri, I always found a job. Even when the children were small, I simply taught night school. I'm sure it was those jobs, that propelled us ahead, provided vacations, allowed us to have the 'finer things' in life, and even got our children through college.

My parents had this idea that you couldn't begin to date until you were 16. How they picked that number out of the hat, I don't know; but that was the deal. One pretty neat thing they did allow us to do was to have occasional parties or dances at the house. We could invite our friends over and dance to our favorite records. Our parents were pretty strict, making us come into the house if it even looked like it was getting dark. As we grew older, they would allow us to sit on the steps with some of our friends a little after dark; so, we were amazed that they would allow us to have dances and parties. I later figured out that they would rather have us in our own house where they could watch us, rather than down the street at "Joe Blow's" house whom they didn't know.

We also learned, later on, that they were surprisingly good dancers themselves; doing their own thing with the Jitterbug, Lindy Hop and the Charleston! Our dances were: The Bop, The Slow Drag, The Cha Cha, The Stroll, The Slop; The Camel Walk and The Strand. Some of our favorite records were: Sixty Minute Man; Come Go with Me; In the Still of the

Night; Lawdy Miss Clawdy; Momma; Do the Huck-a-Buck; and Good Night Sweetheart...

Another source of inexpensive fun was our love of board games, cards and working puzzles. Dad taught us how to play checkers, dominos, pinochle, and poker. Mother liked puzzles and word games. Irma and I liked cross word puzzles and cryptograms. Doris liked Word Find; Chucky, (Homer, Jr.), liked Monopoly and Brenda liked Rummy Cube. We all liked Pokeno. We carried our love of games into our adulthood, and often invited our family and friends over for Game Night.

Walter and Dad playing Checkers

Chapter 3

MY SCHOOLING

I attended all Philadelphia Public Schools, and all of my teachers were white. I never even saw a black teacher, and didn't know that they existed. It amazed me that I wound up being one, and attended a Historically Black College, where the majority of the teachers were black. What irony.

ELEMENTARY SCHOOL: Alcorn Elementary School, 32nd & Dickinson St., Phila., PA **(1941-1949)**

My earliest memory of school was kindergarten. I was about 3 ½ going on 4 years old. Because of the War, (World War II), I was allowed to start school early, since there was a shortage of children during that time. I started kindergarten crying, because I couldn't find an item, the teacher, Mrs. McGraff, asked me to retrieve; and I ended kindergarten crying, because my sister, Doris, was moving on to 1st grade, and I had to remain in kindergarten for another year! Boy, life was hard, I thought!

Things picked up, later on, and I began to enjoy school. In 4th grade I was the teacher's pet, along with my Jewish friend, Rhoda Goldstein. We stayed after school and erased boards, beat the erasers, and helped out as needed. In return we received candy and treats from our teacher, Mrs. Williams. Rhoda and I remained friends through high school. When we came back to our 50th Class Reunion, I asked Rhoda if she remembered being the teacher's pet in 4[th]grade. She said she remembered, and it was her one and only time being one. I told her, me too. We both laughed.

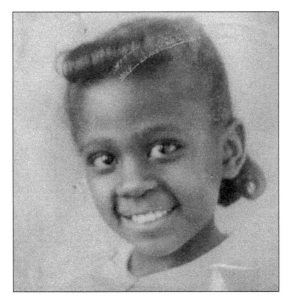

Betty Carolyn, Elementary School

In 6th grade, my teacher, Mrs. DePaul, was asked to send a student down to the office with good handwriting to help out there. After looking over all of her students, I was so proud when she chose me! She was such a great teacher, and I will never forget the unit she taught us on South America. I also remember another incident when she had to stand on a chair in the closet to reach the art supplies for our next lesson. George Williams whistled at her. When she got down and found out who it was, she said, "My goodness, George, I thought I was sweet sixteen again!" We all laughed.

Back in the day, you graduated from 6th grade in elementary school, and went on to Jr. High School; an entirely different school, for grades 7-9. I can still remember the pretty white dress my mother bought me for the closing exercise. My curls were still warm as I scurried to join my classmates and take my seat. The family would come later. I was moving on up to Junior High School! The problem I always had with moving on up, was, that my oldest sister, Irma, was always moving on up too, but to a better grade or situation. For instance, I was going on into junior high school, but she was going on into high school. When I was going on to enter high school, she was going on into college. Of course, mom and dad were always overly excited as she broke new ground. She was the oldest and always the first to do new things. I always seemed to bring up the rear, and my achievements didn't seem as stellar. Bummer!

JUNIOR HIGH SCHOOL: Audenried Jr. High School, 33rd & Tasker St., Phila., PA **(1949-1952)**

Now you're talking a whole new ballgame. What a difference a school makes! The children were older, bigger and more intimidating. Some were physically mature, and some were still scrawny like me. I decided to rise to the occasion and do the best that I could; and besides, my Dad gave us a nickel for every "A" that we made! I was ready!

I made some new friends: Jean, Irene, and Sarah; settled in, and began my junior high school journey. I didn't know it would be such fun. I excelled in athletics (like my Dad); and didn't do too badly academically. I won the 7th grade Spelling Bee, received charms for my bracelet for athletic excellence, won the 8th grade Charter Contest, played piano with the orchestra, danced in a routine on stage, did a high jump exhibition on stage, and ran for School President in 9th grade. Unlike kindergarten, life was great! I forgot about competing with my oldest sister, and decided to just be me, do my own thing, and enjoy the moment.

Just to elaborate on a few things: When I said I played for the orchestra, that meant I played 'my note'. There were three of us on the piano, and each one of us played a note. I guess together we made up a chord. All I know is that it was fun, and I made a life-long friend, Ella Jones. My classmates thought it was cool too.

As for the 8th grade Charter Contest, Philadelphia was in the process of making changes to their Charter. They challenged the Public-School students to gather articles about it, summarize what the article was about, and place the information and articles in a scrapbook. We couldn't afford a scrapbook, so I got a small copybook and entered the contest. Everyone was surprised when my little copybook won, up against large and decorative scrapbooks. I think, while they were concentrating on looks and appearance, I was concentrating on content, and what the judges had asked us to do. My summaries and content were evidently on point, and I believe that is why I won the contest for my 8th grade level.

Betty Carolyn, in the Center

Now about that high jump experience. I was a little tyke just under 5 feet. I had no experience or training, just raw talent, I guess. Most people when they saw me run up to the bar, thought I was going to run under it! I simply ran up to the bar, and then leaped over it. At this particular assembly, the first time, I missed the mark. My skull hit that hardwood floor and I thought I was knocked out for sure. I refused to go out and try again. My head hurt and I was embarrassed. I could just see and hear all of my classmates laughing now. My teachers began talking to me and trying to get me to try again. I wasn't having it. I was done! "Come on, Betty. Try again. You can do it; just like you do in gym!" After much pressure and goading, I reluctantly agreed to try one more time. I cleared the bar to the roar and approval of the crowd! You have to understand that I was only about 4'10" or so, and the bar was set at exactly 5 feet. As I said before, it must have appeared as if I were going to run under the bar and not over it. At any event, I'm glad I made it, so I could have a story to tell my grandchildren!

HIGH SCHOOL: West Philadelphia High School, 47th & Locust St., Philadelphia, PA **(1952-1955)**

Betty Carolyn

You talk about a game changer. High School was definitely it. Everyone seemed so cool and together. I wondered how I would fit in. I gave it my best shot and wound up enjoying myself. My best friend was Jackie Cottman, and we were perfect together. (Opposites, of course.) She dragged me to basketball games when I didn't want to go. We shared lunches and lunch money. Sometimes she would have it and I wouldn't, and vice versa. She was more fun and outgoing; I was more serious, and low key, at this time. I remember her yelling at 'Wilt the Stilt' (later to become the NBA's next 7' draft who became famous and broke all kinds of records); and telling him how unfriendly he was. I was embarrassed. He was from Overbrook High, I think. My other friends included: Mary Rochester, Marie Ball and Shirley Moore.

My biggest interest was sports. My parents both worked, so they encouraged us stay for after school activities. I played softball, volleyball, gymnastics, and everything they offered. Once a year (or semester), the school held gymnastic meets for each grade level. You had to do high performances on the ropes, the swings, the horse, and the boom. I usually won for my grade level. Every now and then, Miriam Moore would take first, and I would take second. I even thought of becoming a gym teacher at one point. Let's explore that thought.

During the 40's and 50's, (and I'm sure even before then), black students weren't encouraged to go into professional careers or high paying jobs. Our Counselors steered us towards the trades and lesser paying jobs; and discouraged us from going to college. I believe that they really believed, that we couldn't do it. Thank God for HBCU's (Historically Black Colleges & Universities), and our parent's insistence.

While in high school, I stayed as active as I was 'allowed'. Case in point, I was not 'allowed' to join the Cheerleading Team; blacks weren't accepted then. So, I filled my time with sports and other after school activities, travelling with the varsity Volleyball Team, playing softball, etc. When I was a senior, I was 'allowed' to be in the 'Mentoring and Guidance Program' for the freshmen class. Another high-light was when I got all A's in Geometry for 2 years in a row. The teachers were thinking about putting me in the gifted and talented program. I quickly squashed that! I think what happened was that I found Geometry chal-lenging. It was like breaking a code and figuring things out, like solving puzzles, which I liked to do. At any event, I enjoyed it tremendously and looked forward to the class. I also had a great teacher, Dr. Kline, who broke things down and challenged us.

Things were going along fine with my best friend, Jackie, until she made this wild suggestion. "Betty, why don't we take up 'Conversational Spanish'?" She didn't get it. I had struggled with Spanish since Junior High School, and finally finished up in High School. I was ecstatic to be done! Take another course? Was she mad? I shut that down in a hurry. Life is funny though. I lived to regret it; especially after America began to become more bi-lingual and many things were written in Spanish. Oh well, live and learn.

Another remembrance of high school that I have was when we felt as if we had a celebrity in our school. Her name was Carolyn Gillespie, and she was the niece of Dizzy Gillespie; now we could name drop. Little did I know that my Uncle, Vernon Isaac, (my father's oldest brother), would one day play saxophone in his band. My dad had nine siblings, and all 10 kids either played an instrument or the piano: Vernon, Clarice, Lincoln, Artis, Eugene, Vernice, Maxine, Enola, & Arthur, Jr. When some of them moved to Philadelphia, dad formed a quartet with two of his brothers, Lincoln, and Eugene, and their first cousin, Hursey Edney. They were really good, and the harmony was tight. They called themselves—"The Oklahoma Wonders" and sang around town and blessed a lot of people. Quartets were "In", back in the day—- The Dixie Hummingbirds, The Five Blind Boys (with Ray Charles), and the Soul Stirrers (with Sam Cook). My dad would bring in quartets and other singing groups to our church... The Davis Sisters, The Porter Singers, and others. Those were really, good times.

THE OKLAHOMA WONDERS

Eugene Isaac, Lincoln Isaac, Hursey Edney, Homer Isaac, Sr. (Dad)

Now back to Uncle Vernon. He was an interesting sort. When he got out of the war, (World War II), he couldn't take America's prejudiced ways any longer, so he and his wife moved to Canada where they became Canadian citizens. He made quite a life and name for himself up there as a professional musician, and started the Montreal and

Ottawa Annual Jazz Concerts, in addition to playing with major bands himself. (Google him for more information.)

Speaking of the war, (World War II), back in the day, they had what was called "The Draft". When young men turned 18, especially if we were at war, you were drafted into the military. You had no choice. Uncle Sam had military posters all around town with a finger pointing and saying, your country needs "You!" All five of my dad's brothers were drafted into the army. My dad always said that his papers must have blown out of the window, because they didn't draft him. We think it was because he was the only son married, and he had 3 kids.

We also thought that they didn't want to take all of his mother's boys into the military, and not leave her with at least one son. Who knows? And since all of his brothers were musical, many of them wound up in "Special Services", playing with the Military Band. His brother, Artis Isaac, made a career of the army, playing the unusual instrument, the glockenspiel, among other instruments.

Last, but not least, while still in high school, we had a chance to be a part of the new latest and greatest television program for teenagers: "American Bandstand", with Bob Horn; later followed by Dick Clark. They taped the show right around the corner from our high school. We hurried over after school to the studio to wait in the long line to try to get in. Notice I said "try"; because they only let so many blacks in per show. When we did make it in, our families were ecstatic, and we felt like celebrities ourselves... dancing on television!

Chapter 4

OUR CHURCH

My parents were church going people, and of course they took us with them. The church was right around the corner, so we didn't have to go far: Williams Temple CME Church, 3133 Reed St., Philadelphia. My parents sang on the choir, taught Sunday School, were Stewards and Trustees and you name it. However, the thing I remember and cherish the most was, singing on the young people's choir, traveling to other churches to sing, and going to our Annual Church Conferences to sing. My dad was the Director, (my sister, Irma, was the organist); and he believed in singing a variety of songs, from gospel to anthems and anything in between. He was always gathering the neighborhood kids to come join the choir. Many of them did, and I'm sure this kept a lot of them constructively engaged and out of trouble.

WILLIAMS TEMPLE CME CHURCH

Top: Betty Carolyn 1st row 3rd one; Bottom: 1st row 5th one

Once a year we would have a Choir anniversary and concert. We had to wear evening gowns and suits and ties. Everyone was encouraged to showcase their talent: solos, musical instruments, piano selections, readings, etc. My sisters and I always did piano solos. This was our home church, and we thoroughly enjoyed our membership.

My older sisters and I had our weddings there. (My brother's wedding was in Mississippi at his wife's church.) All of our children were christened there, too.

I had a rainbow-themed wedding with 6 bridesmaids and 6 groomsmen. It was beautiful. We honeymooned in the Poconos at the lovely black resort, Hillside Inn, (It was the only resort that would let us in). Also, back in the day, the reception was held in the Church Fellowship Hall, followed by a Reception/Party for the young people, usually at a private home, in this case, at my sister Irma's house in West Philly. She and her husband, Henry Parks, also allowed us to stay with them for our first year of marriage while we finished our education at Cheyney University. Family helping family. You can't beat it. Pass it along.

We continued there at Williams Temple until we moved away. In my case, until my husband started his own church. My oldest sister, Irma, remained there, and has been an active member for over 80 years!

My dad used to run trips from the church to ball games and other events. This was always fun, and we used to join him when we could. They were fundraisers for the church, but I'm sure dad got his share of the deals too.

Dad was always bringing singing groups and quartets to our church, as mentioned before, or coming up with some activity to entertain or move the church along. We had raffles, and outings, and programs, and any other creative event they could think of to help the church raise money. These were experiences that I could draw from, later on in life, when I assumed leadership roles in my own church, other clubs, and organizations.

Chapter 5

THE FAMILY

One day my dad came home and plopped a big black instrument on the table. We said, "What is that?" He said, a typewriter. How do you work it or what do we do with it? He said he didn't know, and that we needed to read the manual that came with it. We read the instruction book and took turns doing what it said. We practiced the drills and learned the letters, and by the end of the summer, we were typing away. I was always one to share and encourage others (or play the teacher), so I brought my friends in one by one and taught them how to type too. I don't know about them, but those self-taught typing lessons got me two good jobs: with the city of Phila., and with the federal government!

During our summers off from school, the local library would sponsor a reading contest program. You had to read so many books, say 50 or so, by the end of the summer, and you would be rewarded or recognized and receive a prize; you also had to write a summary to show that you really read the book. This kept us busy and I found it to be fun, since I liked to read. My favorite stories were historical love novels.

Speaking of school, my sister Irma and I liked school; perhaps that was why we both became teachers. (Irma went to Temple, and I went to Cheyney.) It was my understanding that my other siblings didn't care for school that much. I can still hear my mother telling my brother that she couldn't understand how he could fail a subject during the school year, and then she had to pay for him to go to summer school, and he would make an A! I guess some things will always remain a mystery. Nevertheless, we all graduated from college and acquired good jobs. My brother went to Lane State College in TN, and later worked at Wayne State University in Detroit, MI. My sister Doris went into X-ray Technology at Jefferson Medical College in Phila., and my younger sister, Brenda, finished at Delaware State, and climbed the corporate ladder with the government. In our family we were all encouraged to go to college. It was just assumed that after high school, that was what you did. The only question was, where do you want to go and what do you want to do?

My husband always said my parents were ahead of their time, especially my dad! From time to time my dad would say, "I think I'll go visit my mother." This may sound like a simple statement, but the problem was, he lived in Philadelphia and his mother lived in California! Didn't bother him. He would hop on a plane, stay four or five days, visit his mother and siblings who had moved to California from Oklahoma, and then come back home.

He also had the habit of visiting his denominational church, the CME's, when he traveled anywhere out of town. For instance, when he visited my daughters in Minnesota (Linda & Maria), he found his way to the nearest CME Church. He also attended a professional ballgame there, alone, at 80 something years old, without a pre-purchased ticket, and got in!

Mother could hold her own too. She was the busiest woman I ever saw in my life. Not only would she do hair until the midnight hour, but she would cook, sew, iron, make dresses for us, crochet or knit table cloths and other items, can foods for the winter, do our hair, dye dad's hair, and sing solos at the church or on the choir. (The song we liked best was, "I Bowed on my Knees and Cried Holy.) She was a great mother and was always very supportive; whether you skinned your knee or appeared in a program at school, she was always there. When we were little, she would tell us bedtime stories. Our favorite was "The Long Leather Bag". No sooner would she finish telling it to us, then we would beg her to tell it again. (At the request of my daughter, Linda, who liked the story also; it is included at the very end of my book. You can also Google it for other variations.)

Mother didn't have any relatives in Philadelphia; they were all in Oklahoma, Oregon, and California. She had 7 siblings: Leora, Ludella, Gertrude, Ira, OT, John L, and Roger. She often emphasized that we had to stick together because we were all the family she had here in Philadelphia. However, when we were teenagers, her niece, Alene, (Aunt Leora's daughter), came and stayed with us for a couple of years. Also, her nephew, Charles, (Uncle John L's son), breezed through for a little bit after he got out of the service; and her father would come from time to time and stay a little while. Other than that, she had no one. So, when her family did manage to come to see her through the years, they would hug, rock and cry for a long time. We didn't understand it all then. I'm sure there was a lot of history and love that went into those hugs and tears, that we didn't know anything about. We just stood to the side and watched and waited for them to finish; and smiled. We were happy for Mother.

I enjoyed being the baby girl, which meant that I couldn't do as much as the older two, or I was just too little. Worked for me. (Now, can I go out and play?) Mother taught us how to cook, sew, clean, and even taught my older sisters how to do hair. I wanted no part of doing hair; it looked like too much hard work to me. Besides, I'd rather be outside playing, or organizing a game, or bossing people around. I lived to regret this decision. I wound up with two girls who loved to swim!! Now, who was supposed to do their hair when they got out of the pool? Oh, boy!

Well, I graduated from high school. Now what? I applied to several colleges, but didn't get in. One college, which I won't name, actually told me they'd reached their quota of blacks! It's a wonder blacks made it in America because prejudice can tear up your self-esteem.

I found a job in a factory that made bows for shoes. I could tell from the beginning that this was not the job for me. There were two other girls in my section and all they wanted to do on Friday, was to go out and party. After two weeks I quit.

My next adventure was in another factory, but this time they put me in the back office to do clerical work. The white girls were in the front office. I used to have to go through the factory area to get to the back. Most were black workers.

They seemed pleased that one of us had landed a clerk's job. The job was ok, but then came the big white Irish boss who wanted to play games. He would come in and swing my chair around and grin and try to be flirtatious. I wasn't having it; needless to say, this job was short lived too.

I was encouraged by family and friends to take the clerk-typist test for the city of Philadelphia and for the government. I took both. The city came through first and I went to work at city hall. It was a great job in a typing pool, and I loved it. I met and made lots of new friends. During our lunch hour, we would go up into Billy Penn's hat; and also, look at the inner workings of the big clock on top of city hall.

Some friends there introduced me to roller skating, and I took off from there. I had done street skating, but this was different. Back in the day, you didn't just race around the track, you actually danced on your skates to different songs, such as "The Skaters' Waltz". All of this was new to me, but exciting. I introduced my two old high school buddies to skating, Marie and Shirley, and we began to make the rounds to different rinks in and around Phila. We took lessons and mastered the dances. We bought little short skating skirts, our own skates, of course, and a small tin skating box to carry everything around. Those were great fun filled days for my late teens.

Near City Hall was a facility called the USO. We didn't know what it was, so we decided to go in and explore it. We found out that it was a place for military personnel to come and socialize and have a good time. They had weekly dances and encouraged young ladies to attend and participate. This we did; and wound up having a great time and making new friends. My cousin, Betty Jo, even found her a husband there. His name was Joe Dial, and he said he was an Indian (Native American). We just thought he was another light skinned Negro. Come to find out, he really was an Indian, from the Lumbee Tribe in Lumberton, NC. They wound up marrying and raising a family in Philadelphia.

Just as I was getting the hang of city hall, the federal government called me for a job at the Philadelphia Navy Yard in a similar capacity. This was a great opportunity because the government paid more. I said good-by to my new friends and headed for the Navy Yard in South Philly, which was great because I still lived at home there. Here again I met some new friends. One became a life-long buddy, Vernita Watts, and we stayed in touch through the years, even when she married and moved to Rockford, Illinois. Our spirits met and she even liked to roller skate. Our supervisor was Imelda Williams. She was my first encounter with a black professional, personally. She was a great role model and we became friends too.

After several years at the Navy Yard, I had this strong desire to move on to college. (This is an example of waiting for God's timing, and not mine.) I said I would try once more, and this time, apply to a Historically Black College. Cheyney State Teachers' College was close by in Pennsylvania and the tuition was reasonable. I even knew several people from our church who went there.

So, in December of 1957, I traveled to Cheyney State, in Pennsylvania, to take the entrance exam. I arrived early and got situated with all of my sharpened pencils and tools. A while later, and I do mean "late", a group of 3 young men straggled in just before we were to start. One had a conk hairdo (i.e., wavy hair), the next one had on suspenders with pants under his arm pits, and the last one had a decid-edly North Philadelphia stroll! The last one with the stroll, strolled directly over to me and asked to borrow a pencil. I was annoyed, and reluctantly loaned him one. (Imagine, coming to a major test, late and unprepared! Who does that?) Later on, he would ask me did I notice that he was the first one to finish the test and leave? Actually, no; I was busy taking a test! I guess I was supposed to understand that the boy had "potential".

He really did have potential; and was here at Cheyney on a full academic scholarship. I didn't know this early on. All I knew was that he was quite handsome and a good dancer.

He was a commuter and often left campus for work. I lived on campus in the dorms. It was difficult to run into each other. We were eventually introduced by JoAnn Gibson and Barbara Kelly, and later, even shared a class or two. We were quite compatible, and you know what they say...the rest was history. I had met my soul mate...Walter A. McDaniel!

Everyone should fall in love at least once. It's such a great experience!

COLLEGE SWEETHEARTS

Walter and Betty, Freshmen at Cheyney

Chapter 6

CHEYNEY UNIVERSITY

Cheyney University proved to be a wonderful experience and just what I needed. Remember I told you that I had never had a black teacher in my life, and didn't even know they existed. Welcome to a historically black college. I couldn't believe the well-educated, and well-spoken black teachers. I listened in amazement. And when they used a word that I didn't know, I wrote it down and practiced using it myself. In the white public schools, most of us blacks just sat quietly in the back of the class and tried not to be conspicuous, seldom raising our hands. Here in the black college, hands went up, opinions were given, and questions were asked. I couldn't believe it! I had never seen anything like it. The teachers were encouraging and helped you to thrive. I also liked the way they dressed. Professors in suits, women in dresses with matching shoes and jewelry; what a sight to behold! I believe I had found my thing!

Now the students themselves were a different story. I had this preconceived notion about what college kids should look like. (Remember, I had just come from working professionally in corporate America; and was used to dressing up.) I fell short of saying that they should be in suits and ties, but I was not prepared for scruffy sneakers and wrinkled jeans, baggie tops and hoodies. They ran their game down, split verbs, strolled around the campus, and did their thing.

What I didn't know, was, what the teachers saw... diamonds in the rough. By the time they became seniors, they did wear suits and ties, spoke well, carried themselves differently, and were prepared to go out and teach or pursue their careers. I later learned that some became Department Heads, Supervisors, Principals and even Superintendents. At least three others became ministers, besides Walter: Isaac Patterson, Mark Peace, and Joe Patterson. Our first English Major to graduate, Billy Adams, the Editor of the College Newspaper whom I replaced, went on to make his mark in journalism and writing. Another, Ed Bradley, found his way into TV Reporting on 60 Minutes. You talk about not judging a book by its cover; I had fallen into that trap. Let's just call it, immaturity.

The teachers knew as black students we came slightly handicapped and scarred. They took great pains to shape us and teach us things that we probably didn't know, in addition to our lessons. For example, they encouraged us to read a newspaper every day, and how to negotiate the Editorial page, and read and interpret the cartoon. They taught us the correct names of the body parts and told us to get away from the slang terms.

They taught us black history. I can still remember the pain and disappointment on the face of one of our teachers, (Prof. Dudley), when she discovered that no one in the class knew who, Dr. Ralph Bunch was! Then there was "colorful" Dean

Menchan, who spoke at one of our assemblies and told us, "Look to your right at, Johnny; now look to your left at, Mary. Next semester when you come back, Johnny won't be here. He will have 'partied' his way right out of the door!" Later on in his speech he said, "Some people will graduate 'Cum Laude'; some will graduate 'Summa Cum Laude', some will graduate 'Magna Cum Laude'; and still others will graduate, "Thank you, Lordy!" They had their way of saying things. But all of them had the same goal...to help us grow, graduate, and succeed.

My favorite teacher, and mentor, was–Dr. James B. Oliver, of the English department. He was such a great teacher. He was the one who encouraged me to become the Editor of the college newspaper, when the current Editor graduated. I also remember how the two of us wrote on the board together a poem about a snowflake. (Most of the other kids had fallen asleep.) I also remember when I told him I didn't know if I really wanted to be a teacher; because I was very uncomfortable about speaking before people, or a group. This seemed to come naturally to some people, and I didn't have it. He said don't worry about anything like that. What you have to do is, simply be more prepared. Write yourself notes or make an outline. That works just as well. I took his advice and it did work out well for me. I also saw this concept play out in other situations in life, for instance, in preaching. Some preachers could preach up a storm, seldom looking at their notes, if at all. Then you had others who preached from their notes, so strongly and with such passion, that you didn't even know they were reading. (Such was the case with my brother's pastor in Detroit.) Everyone must find their style; and walk in that.

Another struggle I had was trying to remember all of the information that was coming my way. I definitely didn't have a 'photogenic' memory, and it was tough. Cheyney taught us that it wasn't a matter of retaining all of the world's information; but knowing where to go to retrieve it, when needed. This was extremely helpful. They also taught us about keeping our emotions in check, and not to react to everything. First, you should consider the source. Who's bringing you this information? What is their background, education, or purpose? Is it someone who can be trusted, or just someone 'babbling' to be heard? Learn the difference. Emotional people are less believable. They appear to be out of control, as opposed to someone in charge of their words and emotions and are able to calmly give sage advice. I recently heard a speaker say: 'Strength...whispers; whereas Weakness...screams!' Pick your battles. Stay calm.

Later on, after I became a teacher at Shoemaker Jr. High School in Philadelphia, I was assigned a student teacher from Cheyney. Guess who her college advisor was? Dr. Oliver. When he came to evaluate her, it was a great reunion, and a pleasure to meet up with him again. We caught up on old times, and he was pleased that I was doing so well.

Betty and Dr. Oliver

While I was at Cheyney, having the best grades in my class, I was selected to be the Homecoming Queen for the freshman class. I also worked for the Dean of Admissions, since I had a clerical background; I was also awarded the 'Phi Beta Sigma Award in Journalism'; and was selected to be the Editor of the College Newspaper my Senior year. My family would drive up to see me some weekends and bring me my favorite donuts. Mother would also do my hair. (Remember, I couldn't!)

Walter and I became engaged unofficially with his fraternity pin; and married in our junior year. He had pledged Phi Beta Sigma, a new Fraternity brought to the college by the Professor of Music, D. Jack Moses. They made a great line and were the talk of the campus.

PHI BETA SIGMA FRATERNITY

Walter, 1st row 3rd from left

Originally, Cheyney offered only three options: Elementary Education, Home Economics, and Industrial Arts Education. We were in Elementary Education. Around my Jr. year, they introduced Secondary Education. I switched over and majored in English. I wound up with a minor in Elem. Ed., and a major in Secondary Education/English.

After high school, while I was working, I had saved up my money, just in case I decided to go to college. That being said, I was able to pay my own tuition for the first 3 semesters. I ran out of money for my fourth semester, so my mother and sister, Irma, stepped in and paid it. After that, Walter and I got married, and he likes to say that he became my

'Scholarship', since he was now working nights at the post office. I tried to tell him that I was helping out too. I worked in the Dean's Office and got paid a grand total of 65 cents an hour! I believe he said, hmm.

Cheyney was such a great college and exposed you to so much. I remember In Sociology class, how they described what a ghetto was, and most of us were offended because that was where we grew up. They described the drunk on the street, the weekly fights on Friday night, playing numbers, street gangs, etc. We just took those things in stride, as part of the happenings, because we saw those things daily on our streets at home. We never looked on our neighbors as impoverished or living in dire straits. It was simply our neighborhood.

They also helped us to bring out our own gifts and talents. I had no idea that I was or could be a gifted writer. No one ever told me so; or trained me in this area. With Cheyney's teaching and encouragement, I learned that I could not only write essays and assignments, but prose, literature, and poetry. I was shocked; but pleased.

Then they talked about corporal punishment. Most of us had been spanked, as kids, and thought nothing of it. If you were bad, you were bad, and got your bottom spanked for it. The Professor's question was, did we turn out Okay <u>because</u> of the spankings, or, <u>in spite of them</u>? We all said, hmm.

We didn't know. All I knew for sure was that children had to be trained. When we raised our own kids, we had a 4-step method. We would talk to them first, next we might have to raise our voice, thirdly there was punishment or withdrawing of privileges, and lastly, it was, 'Bring out the belt!' I was determined not to physically correct my kids as often as I had been spanked. Children are all different, though, and respond to correction differently. We did what worked for us; and besides, there was the Biblical model for us Christians:

> **Proverbs-19:18**...Chasten thy son while there is hope; and let not thy soul spare for his crying.

> **Proverbs-22:15**...Foolishness is bound in the heart of a child; but the rod of correction shall drive it far from him.

> **Proverbs-23:13**...Withhold not correction from the child; for if thou beatest him with the rod, he shall not die.

There are more scriptures, but I think you get the idea. Even non-Christians know there comes a point when you have to correct a child. They have to be trained. It's like when you go into the military. You don't know how to be a soldier; you have to be trained. It's the same with children; you have to train and teach them how to become responsible adults. How do you do it? That's between you and your God.

I remember one time when our kids were little, Walter and I were in the kitchen when we heard this loud crash in the living room where the children were playing. We ran in and saw our large round glass coffee table broken. After checking everybody to make sure they were ok, we asked, who did it? Six eyes rolled up and looked at the ceiling in inno-cent complicity. Since no one would confess, all six eyes got a spanking and a lecture on not destroying house property.

After I became an adult and a parent, and my dad was old and gray; I asked him if he thought he gave us too many spankings when we were kids? He said, "I don't remember any of that. You all turned out perfect?" It was my turn to say, hmm.

Chapter 7
AFTER COLLEGE

Walter went to summer school and accelerated his schooling at Cheyney, graduating in 3 years. I came out in 4. After we graduated, we moved into our own apartment, after staying with my sister, Irma, for a while. We both acquired teaching jobs and were on our way.

We offered Walter's sister, Phyllis, the opportunity to go to college as we did, and we would pay her tuition. She declined. She had a good job with the city of Philadelphia and had 3 boys to raise. After her kids were grown and she had put them through school, she then went back to school herself. She went to Temple University, made all "A's", and continued and got her Masters. What wisdom taught us was that there is what is called a state of 'readiness', and people cannot or will not move forward until they are ready, or until God gives them the green light. Nevertheless, we were just glad that she moved on, and did well. His other sister, Mira, went to school at Lincoln University in PA, and Columbia University in New York.

I also remember a time after I graduated and got a good teaching job, that I ran into a former student from Cheyney. I was waiting for a bus to take me to work, (dressed to the "nines", as Cheyney had taught us), when she walked by. I recognized her immediately and we struck up a conversation.

I remember her being very smart and a good student. She dropped out around our junior year and I never saw her again until now. She seemed glad to see me, and we talked extensively and reconnected. Years later I ran into her again, and she told me that after talking with me, she went back to Cheyney and finished. I was happy for her, and glad I was able to help. Never underestimate the power of encouraging words.

Uncle Sam was the great interrupter for us, and drafted Walter in 1962. After a year and a half of teaching, I decided to join him where he was stationed at Fort Leonard Wood, Missouri. It started off as a horrible experience because the hotel where Walter had booked me, refused to give me a room because I was black; or as they put it, they were all filled up. I was in tears as I waited for Walter to come and get me, and as I watched others (all white), check in after me. You have to remember that this was in the 60's, and prejudice was at its height: there were separate water fountains; you had to sit in the back of the bus; and obviously, there was no checking in at upscale hotels, etc. They definitely didn't care that my husband was in the military, serving and defending this country! Walter finally arrived and haggled with them, and they sent us down the road to another hotel; but I was really angry with them, and it left a bitter taste in my spirit.

Things picked up later on, when the Lord blessed me with a job on the army base at the elementary school there. After his two years were up in the military, we moved back to Philadelphia, in 1964.

When we returned from MO, my dad and the music teacher from Shoemaker Jr. High School, (where my sister,

Irma, was teaching), Verolga Nix, joined together and formed the "Methodian Concert Choir". Their goal was to bring good music to the community and to preserve the Negro Spiritual, (similar to the group, 'The Wings Over Jordan'). I quickly joined and was blessed by my tenure. We traveled extensively, sang at many churches, appeared on radio and television, produced an album, and offered an alternative to the music of the day. One big highlight of the group was when we took a tour from coast to coast, traveling from Philadelphia to California, and we were the second black choir to sing at the Mormon Tabernacle Cathedral, in Salt Lake City, Utah.

THE METHODIAN CONCERT CHOIR

Betty, 5th from the left, next to Irma on right

Verolga was a talented, and gifted musician. She could hear notes, teach harmony lines, interpret and creatively present her songs, play the piano, and direct. Sometimes she would rehearse us in quartets (soprano, alto, tenor and base) to see if you could hold your line. We were also trained to blend with others and memorize our music. Our signature song was, the spiritual/anthem, "Soon I Will Be Done"; and our most challenging song was, "Ezekiel Saw the Wheel", sung in eight-part harmony (1st and 2nd soprano, 1st and 2nd alto, etc.). I hated to see this chapter of my life 'end'; but starting and raising a family, and other obligations, caused many of us to discontinue. I understand that she re-organized under the name of 'The Intermezzos', and continued on, traveling throughout the US and Europe.

Walter and I found teaching jobs and began to save so we could buy our own house and start our family. We bought a home in a beautiful section of Philadelphia, that we didn't even know existed, Mt. Airy. Little did we know that the realtor was using us as "Block Busters" to break up the neighborhood, until the whites began to move out, and neighbors kept asking me whose house was I cleaning for? We did not let these distractions deter us. We were on a mission and wanted the best for our family. That was on them if they didn't want to stick around and see what kind of people we were, but only saw the hue of our skin. Besides, my parents raised me to understand that I was as good as anybody else, and I could do like anyone else!

Life is funny. We thought we could simply say, "Let's have a family", and presto, it would happen. Life was saying, not so fast. We had been married for 7 years, before our bouncing little girl, Linda Louise, came into the world. She loves to tell the story of how we, 'left her' at the hospital, because we were busy putting cards, gifts and balloons into the car and were ready to pull off, when the nurse said, "You-hoo! Are you forgetting something?"; as she handed us our "Bundle of Joy!"

During the 7 years interim before we had kids, here we were in this big house in Mt. Airy. Walter determined that I needed something to do, some other project, "other than him." He was getting his 'Masters' in Research and Statistics at Lehigh University in Pennsylvania, and I was teaching at Shoemaker Jr. High School in West Philadelphia. There were a lot of young teachers and professionals just starting out like me. I came up with the idea of starting a lady's club. We could fellowship together, take trips together, celebrate holidays together, and meet monthly at each other's home and share our cooking skills and recipes. The idea caught on and we formed the "Las Damas" lady's club in 1966. This fellowship continued for over 50 years, and we still meet today from time to time for special outings or celebrations. There remains 5 Charter members, including myself: Hattie Cruger, Betty Brennan, Emma Dickerson and Melva Brown. We have had upwards of 20 members or more, at one time, not counting the husbands who say they were members too, having labored along with us during this journey; also, there were many more members who had come and gone.

LAS DAMAS LADIES CLUB

50TH ANNIVERSARY

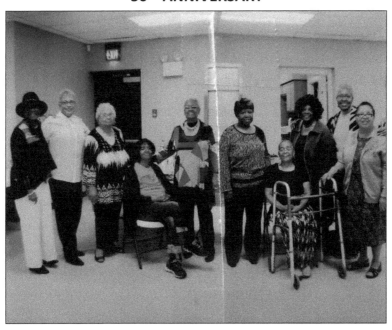

Betty, 5th from Left

Early on, Walter and I had opted to try all life had to offer. We wanted to engage in as many new and challenging experiences as we could. During our lifetime, not necessarily in this order, we tried: Ice skating, roller skating, skiing, tennis, golf, horseback riding, Ballroom Dancing, violin lessons, calligraphy, arts and crafts, cake decorating, the Stock Market, betting at the race track, stocks and bonds, CD's, Mutual Funds, and good old fashion savings accounts. The point is, don't settle in on one or two things. Try different things. You just may find your niche. Life is short. Enjoy it while you can.

Walter and I were also what you would call 'independent spirits', meaning, if you wanted to do something and others wanted to come along too, fine; if not, it was still fine; we'd simply go it alone. Even as kids, we didn't need a mob of friends to verify us or give us approval. We had no problem with leaving the crowd behind, especially if they were simply going to hinder, and not help, or not add something to the mix. All we needed, besides family, was a couple of good honest friends who had your back. Some people needed a mob around them at all times. This was not for us. I guess we were more what you call 'private people', very independent and self-sufficient; and felt that if you wanted a job done right, many times you had to do it yourself! It took a lot of learning and growing to begin to let others in and learn to trust them. I believe that growing up in the ghetto, and living in a hostile environment, taught us to always be cautious; so, you see, we still had a lot more to 'untangle' in life.

I had always wanted 4 children, 2 girls and 2 boys, so everyone would have someone to play with. After the wicked labor pains and the awful stress of physically having a baby, I was ready to hang it up with an only child (like my sister, Irma, who had one child, Kimberly). I felt bad, so I considered one more. 15 months later, Paul Walter Lee McDaniel made his entrance into the world. Pain, pain, pain; more yelling, more stress. I knew this was it. A girl and a boy too! We're done here! While I was trying to figure out how to 'shut this ship down', so to speak, and call it a day, you guessed it, Maria Antoinette McDaniel made her grand entrance. It was almost as if the Lord was saying, oh, you haven't lived, until you've had a Maria Antoinette; and besides, she's the one who's going to give you all of those grandchildren! The children were all about a year and a half apart, and it felt like I had triplets. I always had two in diapers at the same time. What a challenge! I now had something to do.

BETTY'S "TRIPLETS"

Linda, Paul & Maria

The Lord was right. The children and the grandchildren have been a blessing; it was just the unbearable delivery pain! Some people are built for pain and others are not. I was not!

I remember when we lived in South Philly, the neighbor across the street from us had a baby every 9 months, or at least, one a year. I think she wound up with about 18 children. She would happily sit on her steps and braid the girls' hair as if she didn't have a care in the world. (Don't forget, these were 5-room houses too!) God bless her soul.

I heard another story of a woman who had 15 or 16 children. Someone asked her, which one was her favorite? She wisely said, "The one who's sick; the one who's in between jobs; the one who's clawing their way through college; etc., etc..." As Cheyney would say, I tucked this gem of wisdom away into my "Intellectual arsenal of weapons!"

This wise mother's wisdom reminds me of what's happening today in America, with the "Black Lives Matter" movement. Critics say, why zero in on black lives, when ALL lives matter. I agree 100% that ALL lives matter; even the 'Good Book' tells us that. But like the wise mother with the 15-16 children implied, sometimes, one child may need a little bit more than the others, at certain times in their lives. Case in point. Right now, in America, it's not the Irish, not the Italians, not other immigrants, but black and brown citizens who are being unjustly targeted by the police: shot in the back, held in choke holds, and being killed. I was so encouraged when, not only people in America rose up and demonstrated against these terrible acts, but people around the world joined them in protest against these inhumane acts against humanity! Life itself matters; and should not be selectively tampered with!

I didn't believe in 'favorites'. I used to tell my son, Paul, he was my 'favorite' son. He would beam and smile with pleasure. When he got a little older, he said, but Mom, I'm your <u>only</u> son! I told him but he was still my 'favorite' son; and Linda was my 'favorite' oldest, first-born daughter; and Maria was my 'favorite' baby girl. (I think he said, hmm.)

(Read Gen., Ch. 37), for more on the effects of 'favorites'; and the book on 'Birth Order' by Kevin Leman, is enlightening, also). Favorites are different from those needing special care and consideration, at certain times in their lives. Favorites go on and on; and expect special treatment <u>all</u> the time...just because.

WALTER'S SIBLINGS

Walter's brother, **Harry**, and his wife, **Lorene**, had 10 children.

Boys in the back: Ronnie, Warren, Danny and Harry, Jr.
Girls: Neetsie, Kitty Kat, Carolyn, Nina, Patricia & Sheila

His older sister, **Phyllis**, had three boys.

Top row: Neil & David
Bottom: Melvin & Phyllis

His baby sister, **Mira**, did not have children.

Mira McDaniel
*His first cousin, Allen Anderson, (Aunt Maggie's son), was raised with the family as the second brother. He later married, Alice Scales, and had two children: Allen, Jr., and Renay.

BETTY'S SIBLINGS

My oldest sister, Irma, had one daughter, Kimberly.

Irma & Kim

My next to the oldest sister, **Doris** had 2 children:
Lee and Lenee.
(And tons of foster children.)

Doris, Lee & Lenee

My baby sister, **Brenda**, had no children.

Brenda Isaac

My brother, **Homer, Jr**. (Chuck) and his wife, **Lyn,** had 2 children, Homer, III (Trey), & daughter, Keysha. Let me tell you a funny story about my brother. Since he worked at Wayne State University in Detroit, his children were eligible to go to the college, free! Where did they go? Michigan State University; Western Michigan University; & Eastern University. Oh well, no free tuition for them!

Homer, Jr. (Chuck) & Homer, III (Trey)
Keysha & Lyn

Chapter 8

WE BEGIN OUR ODYSSEY

I n 1972, we got a bit restless with Phila., and wanted to move around a bit. I had family in California and liked the warm weather out there. Walter wanted to move to his hometown in Morganton, North Carolina and relive some of his fond memories there. He also had family still there, including his mother.

We moved to California first, where I taught for a while at a middle school in L.A. I also got involved in jewelry sales. I gave jewelry parties and demonstrations at various ladies' homes. Also, while there, I entered a 'Black History' writing Contest for the newspaper; and won the winning essay. If I recall correctly, I believe I likened George Washington to George Washington Carter, Benjamin Franklin to Benjamin Banneker, etc., etc. I won a trip to Hawaii.

LA Mayor Bradley presenting
Winning Ticket to Hawaii to Betty

I also directed a choir there and became active in my grandmother's church. I trained other women in the jewelry business; and rose to be Area Director for Celebrity Fashion Jewels. We bought a duplex home, or as they say in California, two on a lot; and we stayed in one house; and rented the other one out.

In 1974, we moved to Walter's hometown, Morganton, North Carolina. This time I got a job at the elementary school there, and Walter got a job in statistics and evaluation at a boys' facility there. Later, a better job in his field came open at a community college in Whiteville, North Carolina. We moved there, and here again the Lord blessed me with a teaching job at the school where the children would attend. I ran the Reading Lab there, and it was a joy to see a non-reader become a reader. Maria, my youngest, was only four at the time, but she insisted that I teach her how to read too; so, I did. I also wrote a book of poetry for children while there.

The Family in North Carolina
Linda, Maria, Betty, Walter & Paul

We started a gospel choir while in Whiteville, North Carolina, called "The Third World Choir". It was amazing how this choir took off. The Lord really blessed us as we sang all around town, and at various churches.

Another remembrance I have is when Walter was called into the ministry. The pastor at St. James AME Church in Whiteville, North Carolina, allowed him to preach his 'Trial Sermon' there. Both of our families came down for this momentous occasion. Also, during this time, that same pastor, Rev. McIntyre, found out that I used to play the piano, and conned me into playing for the church. I tried to tell him that I hadn't played in years, and never for a church. His thing was that they didn't have anyone at the time, and it would be a great help and blessing if I would consider playing for them. I told him my sister, Irma, was the pianist in our family. But, as he said with a smile, but your sister isn't here. It's just you. I said, ugh! So, I practiced and practiced and got in shape, and learned how to play gospel music and hymns. I really didn't think it was my gift; because I couldn't pick up a song and play it without music. They didn't care. They were pleased to finally have someone. When I arrived for rehearsal, they were already seated, three rows deep, ecstatic to finally have someone. They didn't care that I had to read the notes. Just read them and play!

Also, while we were in Whiteville, a lovely Christian family from the church, the Johnsons', "adopted" us. They already had 9 or 10 children of their own, and we made 15! They had us over for dinner, gave Walter his own pig, and even offered us several of their many acres so that we could settle on it, if we wanted to. I also admired the way the grown children who had moved away to northern cities, would come home at harvest time, and help their dad with the cropping. What a great example of a Christian family! The youngest daughter, Ida Sue, has remained in touch with us through the years.

Chapter 9

MAYS LANDING, NJ

In 1977, we moved back East to Mays Landing, New Jersey, where Walter acquired a job at Atlantic Community College, still in research. I found a teaching job in Atlantic City, teaching Adult Basic Education. I was also offered a job with the Atlantic City daily newspaper; but declined, due to the long hours, and I would be working at night.

The next year a job in English (my major), came open at Oakcrest High School, in Mays Landing, NJ. I quickly applied for it; and wound up staying there for 5 years, until the school split with Egg Harbor Township. I then went to Egg Harbor Twp. High School, and stayed there until my retirement in 1992, exactly 30 years from when I first started teaching in 1962. Before I retired, I went on Sabbatical Leave in 1988, and taught for one year at Camden County Community College. That made my teaching career complete. I had run the gamete: Elementary School; Junior High School; High School; Adult Basic Education; and Community College. During my teaching tenure, I worked with the Drama Club, started a Gospel Choir, worked with their newsletter, and at one time, served as Asst. Chairperson for the English Department.

Around 1978, a friend of mine, Dianne Partee, shared with me that the Philadelphia School District was looking for someone to write a workbook for the students, on their level, and that would meet their needs in Social Studies. I accepted the challenge and wrote a workbook on, "The Environment", which dealt with communities around the world. The book also contained puzzles and games to supplement the content. Twenty public schools and five parochial schools used the booklet in their classrooms to broaden their lessons and afford the students some variety.

**Betty published book on "Environment" for
Public and Parochial Schools of Philadelphia**

While we were in Mays Landing, we affiliated ourselves with the St. James AME Church in Atlantic City, where Rev. William Cody was the Pastor. He took Walter on as an Associate Pastor and got him ordained. He was assigned to a church in Wildwood, NJ–Asbury AME Church, where he stayed for 2 years. Many thanks to member, Estelle White, who opened up her home and her heart to us, since we lived out of town, and had to spend entire days at church or ministering to others there in Wildwood.

Sis. Betty McDaniel & Sis. Estelle White

His second assignment was to Mt. Zion AME Church in Woodstown, NJ., where he stayed for 2 years before he began his own church in Sicklerville, NJ.

Paul, Betty, Linda, Maria & Walter

Around 1978, while still living in Mays Landing, I was, "Born Again"! My sister-in-law, Phyllis Rowden's Pastor, Rev. Benjamin Tolbert, one day looked me in the eye and asked me if I were "Saved"? I knew what that meant, but I wasn't sure, so I muttered a couple of generic phrases like, 'I hope so; I'm working on it; I've been in the church a long time, etc., etc.' He continued to look me in the eye and said, 'If you were saved, you should not hesitate. You should know it beyond a shadow of a doubt, and be able to recite supporting scriptures, such as: (Romans 3:23; 5:8; 6:23; 10:09; & 10:13); and also—(John 3:16, and Acts 16:31).

After that, I made sure that I said the "Sinner's Prayer" to myself, every time I heard the call to salvation at a church. I learned the salvation scriptures. I felt better. I felt saved. I told the Lord that it had been a while since I had learned the books of the Bible and read it; and that I would need some help to get back involved again. God is so faithful. From that day forward, and for a solid year...every time I was in church and the minister said to turn to a 'particular scripture', I would simply open my Bible and the scripture would be right there! It got to be a little scary sometimes, but I knew it was the Lord working and answering prayer. I also developed a strong desire to study the word of God, so I sought out as many Bible Studies as I could find; and began to learn and grow.

Once you belong to the Lord, you belong to Him, and cannot go back to your old ways. There was a time when I went to the Teachers Convention in Atlantic City. A teacher had chartered a bus for us; and explained that if we paid $25.00 for the ride, we could get that back at the Casino, once we got there. Another teacher and I sat up front near the door, so that we would be the first to get off the bus and run and claim our money back. When we arrived, we scurried quickly off the bus and raced through the casino to redeem our tickets.

I thought things had gone pretty well; until the convention was over, and I left to meet the bus for my ride back. No sooner did I leave the casino, when "Acid Rain" came down from the heavens and blinded my eyes and disorientated me! I began stumbling...and couldn't see. It didn't hurt, but it was unnerving, and no one else seemed to be affected, but me! I barely made it to the bus stop, but the bus had gone. I had to call home for a ride; and had to wait for several hours in one of those unsavory bus-shelter stops, with derelicts and homeless people giving me the eye. It would be years before I would set foot into a casino again, and many more years before I understood why I was so chastened by the Lord. I fell under the scripture in (Proverbs 6:16-19) that tells of the seven things that the Lord hates; one of which is, "Feet that be swift in running to mischief." I was done!

Most people I knew grew up in what is called "Carnal Churches," meaning we were Christians and believed in Christ, but we were never taught How to be a Christian. We knew the basics: don't kill, don't lie, don't cheat, don't steal, etc. But how do you love your enemy? How can you even love your neighbor as yourself? And what was this talk about tithing and giving 10% of your income? I can barely feed myself and my family! Then I haggled over whether to tithe off of my gross pay, or off of my net. I thought it should be off of the net. My thing was, you can't tithe off of something that you don't get. Someone asked me, does Uncle Sam get his percentage off of the net? No, he goes right to the top, your gross pay. Besides, scripture says to bring the Lord your "First Fruit". I said, ugh!

Thank God I grew and changed. The key was to really study the Bible, and purpose in your heart to do what it says. For those of you struggling with the tithing concept, go to (Mal. 3:8-10). God promises you a lot of good things when you are obedient in this area. As a matter of fact, He actually challenges you to do so; then He can show you how He will pour out his blessings upon you. You will begin to see the Lord work in your life and prove himself over and over again, that His word is true, He loves you, He will do for you, and He will always be advocating for you. Didn't He die for you? Find yourself a good biblical church that teaches and lives the word.

Some of my other spiritual experiences included: Speaking in tongues, being slain in the Spirit, being warned of imminent danger, and the Lord speaking to and singing to my spirit. I also remember the time when I fell asleep at the wheel of my car driving home from work one day; when all of a sudden, "Someone", began to shake me violently. I was getting an attitude, wondering who would wake me so roughly from such a sound sleep. I opened my eyes and saw that I had drifted onto the other side of the road headed towards an embankment! Needless to say, I quickly self-corrected, and proceeded to thank the Lord all the way home! (Psalm 91:11-12), tells us how 'He will give his angels charge over us, lest we dash our feet against a stone'.

Sometimes we look at people who call themselves Christians, and we are appalled at some of the things that they do, or don't do. Here's a thought for you. Rather than judge them harshly, just remember that we are all not on the same level of spiritual growth. Some are just beginning in their faith, and some have studied and are more mature in their faith. The question is not about them, but what will you do with your faith?

Another lesson I learned in life dealt with that of the work ethic. How many times have we had a boss or supervisor whom we thought did everything wrong, or who was mean and/or unreasonable? Or a company that was doing things incorrectly in your eyes, and you had a better way or plan, and they simply weren't listening or interested. Here's the key: As long as you're working for them, and they are paying you, do things their way and give them what they want. As one wise pastor once said (Rev. McDaniel), as long as it's not...

*Immoral

*Illegal...or

*Injurious to your health

Do what they say. Let them run their company the way that they want to. If it's too unbearable, (and you are tired of taking their money), you have three options:

—Change your attitude; it is what it is

—Change your job; find one more to your liking

—Change your career; start your own business

(Just a word from the wise in passing.)

Finally, let me share with you a Scripture that has blessed me and carried me through the years: (Colossians, 3:23). Whether it's on the job, holding an office, raising children, or just doing a small task, this scripture applies to everything you do, and will keep you focused and on the right track! Look it up; memorize it; hold it close to your chest. It will bless and encourage you, over, and over again.

Chapter 10
SICKLERVILLE, NJ

We moved to Sicklerville, NJ, in August 1979, where I told my family that I was through with my odyssey and moving around. Just bury me in the back yard. I kept my word and we have lived in the same house for over 40 years.

Betty in front of house in Sicklerville

Sicklerville was a great place to raise the children. I had promised my son, Paul, that once we got there, if there were no boys his age, I might consider having one more son. He joined me in knocking on doors and introducing ourselves and getting to know our neighbors. Thank God he found some new friends: Aaron, BJ, Billy, Byron, and a host of others; not to mention those friends he made at school and through the different sports and activities.

The children were encouraged to take musical lessons and to play one instrument in addition to the piano. Linda chose the clarinet, Paul, the saxophone, and Maria the flute. They interchanged their instruments; and wound up being able to play 3 different ones. When we went to hear them play in the band one day, Paul came out with yet a different instrument, (other than what we were paying for). He was playing the trombone now. His thing was that the Band Teacher, Mr. Tweed, needed trombonists and he volunteered. How about telling your parents?!

Piano lessons were another story. Lessons were on Friday evening. When I came home from work, they were all fighting to get to the piano and practice. My thing was, what happened to Sat. through Thur.? At any event, I saw that they weren't serious, so I was prepared to cut off these lessons. Maria was the only one who said if I changed the piano teacher, she would continue. We found her a new teacher and she went on to become quite proficient at it, even playing for our church choir, later on. They all were good at music, not just the piano. Linda could sing a great alto line, and Paul had a strong baritone voice. He could also memorize his band music, while others struggled to read it. Maria sang 2nd soprano, and also played the piccolo. They all had a natural gift for harmonizing and singing together, or in the choir. They all continued with their instruments through high school.

We lived next door to a playground, so that was a plus, except when I needed to call them in to eat or do a chore. Sometimes I had to call Paul by his full name to get him off the basketball court—— Paul Walter Lee McDaniel... of course his friends teased him, and he was embarrassed.

They navigated school pretty well. Maria went into the gifted and talented classes. Linda was encouraged to take up electives in addition to her college prep classes, such as typing and cosmetology. Paul majored in 'Break Dancing' and 'Spinning on his Head', although he did manage to become Class President in his Senior year because of his popularity. He was more into socializing with people and having a good time, than into his academic studies.

Linda told us that she had been bullied in high school. I'm sure it was because she was meek and mild and had a warm, quiet spirit. She was also very pretty and had a giving heart. This was hard for me to see, since I was just the opposite as a kid: aggressive, in your face, competitive, and didn't mind fighting. Maria, on the other hand, was physically small, but didn't mind holding her own either. Other than that, the children were quite involved in their high school. They loved the Band Competition with other schools. We always attended and cheered them on. Paul also sang with the school choir. All of them participated in sports: basketball, track, gymnastics, tap dancing, softball, etc. The girls were always receiving awards in academics, honor roll, or on the Principal's List.

I remember the time when Paul told us that we had to come to the school because he was going to receive a trophy. Being the supportive parents that we were, Walter and I took off from work to attend his assembly. When they called his name, the kids stood on their feet and cheered loudly; we did too. He came out, the music started, and he began his routine. He began to Break Dance, spin on his head, and the crowd went wild with approval. The boy could really dance, but...hmm. They gave him a trophy for the 'Best Break Dancer' in the school. No comment...

We were active in our community. We organized our development, Primrose Gate, to incorporate a town watch and neighbors helping neighbors. We would hold meetings in the playground once or twice a month. We held a Bible Study on the playground premises and offered a game day. We wanted to lend our presence and combat any crime or drug movement that might be creeping into the park.

I loved the way most residents kept their property up and families were encouraged to move in. Renters and foster care were not prevalent at the time, although they eventually crept in. Gangs and graffiti were not welcomed at all, and we tried to keep our neighborhood as safe as possible, and a place where one desired to live.

We put in a swimming pool so our children and their friends would have a fun activity to do in the summer. The kids love to tell the story of how they learned how to swim. It was back in North Carolina at the recreation center. Their daddy threw them into the pool, one by one, and barked instructions from the side about kicking and moving their arms and body. They say they were traumatized, but they did learn to swim. (I'm glad I wasn't there. I would have been traumatized too.) And since our back yard was so large, we also added a basketball half court, volleyball, and put out picnic tables. We screened in the back-patio area and created an indoor/outdoor room for eating and fellowship. The children (and adults) loved it, and spending time out back was one of our fondest memories. We also held birthday parties, and anniversaries, and church functions out there too.

Lee Paul Jay

Maria & Lenee

The pool and the patio room
At table: Lori, April & Melissa

We also had a 5-bedroom house, so guests and friends were always welcomed and allowed to stay over. We met life-long neighbors like Leon and Joyce James; Bill and Debbie Hicks; The Foats; The Crosby's; The Browns; etc. Now you see why I didn't want to move. I know a good blessing when I see one.

Also, in raising the kids, we had certain 'Pat Answers' for certain things. For instance:

*This is not a restaurant. You will eat what is placed before you.

*I don't care what Johnny's parents permit; we can only raise you.

*Peer pressure? You be the peer pressure and pressure others to do what is right!

* I can't do this; I can't do that. Well, you can't have all of the gifts. You can't just be pretty, handsome, a writer, an athlete, etc. Let others have their gifts too!

I think they got the idea.

Chapter 11

THE CHILDREN'S LEGACY

A quick summary of the children. They all graduated from Edgewood Senior High School in Winslow Township, New Jersey in succession: Linda, in 1986; Paul, in 1987; and Maria, in 1988, (having gone to Summer School, and graduating a year early).

THE CATHIE FAMILY

Linda, Doug & Jarrel Cathie

Linda did her undergraduate work at Norfolk State University in Virginia, where She got her B. S. Degree in Mass Communication. This was followed by a Masters' Degree, in Special Education and Learning Disabilities (M.ED.) at the University of Minnesota. While in MN, she wrote and produced a play at an area theater. The family flew out to support her. She then matriculated to the University of Virginia where she received her Doctorate in Special Education, (Ph.D.)

She is currently employed as a Learning Consultant on the Child Study Team at Winslow Township High School in NJ (her former high school), where she advocates for students with special needs, interprets the applicable laws concerning them to administrators and teachers, plans appropriate accommodations and programs for them, supports teachers, and consults with and keeps the parents apprised.

She was active in her church, Faith United, and was well known for her annual production of the Candlelight Christmas Eve Service, where she sponsored many gifted and talented artists from the area, and always presented the Gospel Story in a new and creative way. Additionally, she sang on the choir, led the Praise Team, was the Church Clerk, Secretary to the Women's Fellowship and to the Board Meetings. She started a Christian Book Club, which is still active to this day.

She is married to George Douglas Cathie, who has one son, Jarrel Cathie. They live here in Sicklerville, NJ.

THE PAUL MCDANIEL FAMILY

Paul & Diane McDaniel, & Imani

After graduating from high school, Paul attended Camden County Community College, in NJ; and Barber Scotia College, in NC. He recently graduated from the University of Phoenix, with a major in Communications and Technology, and is currently teaching in Florida.

He is also an ordained Minister, like his father. While working with his dad in ministry at Faith United Christian Church, in Berlin, NJ, he was the Associate Pastor, sang on the choir, taught classes, counseled, preached, and helped out as needed in all areas.

While in High School, he was very active in sports, and played on the basketball team. He was in the band and sang with the choir. He was also very sociable, and well liked, and was elected Class President his senior year.

He has directed several plays, made videos, and produced an independent film, called "Spiricide". While in the military, he excelled in Morse Code and received recognition for his outstanding performance. He was stationed in South Carolina, Florida and Maryland. He is currently married to Diane Mmari McDaniel from Tanzania, Africa. He gave me my first granddaughter, Imani Buckmon McDaniel.

THE DANIEL FAMILY

Valdon, II & Maria
Valdon, III, Ananda, & Aliyah

Maria did her undergraduate studies at Spelman College in Atlanta, Georgia. She was active in Morehouse College's

Band Front. She majored in law and computer science. (Oprah Winfrey was her Commencement Speaker, '93).

After graduating, she worked for a time in Minnesota where she was crowned 'Miss Black Minnesota' in 1993; and was also crowned, 'Miss Talent' and 'Miss Congeniality'. She went on to the 'Miss Black USA' Pageant in Washington, DC., and placed in the top 10.

She received her Juris Doctorate Law Degree from Rutgers University in Camden, NJ.

She practiced law as a Public Defender early on, and later taught Law at Philadelphia Community College for over 10 years. She has published 3 law books, and numerous law articles.

She is the Founder and Artistic Director of the 'iDance Ministry' that runs out of Virginia, New Jersey, Pennsylvania, and New York. She is active in her church; and teaches Law at Southern New Hampshire University. She stays active in her community and recently appeared on a virtual online panel about the killing of George Floyd, police brutality, and the racial upheaval that was going on at the time.

She gave me 3 grandchildren: Aliyah Niara, Ananda Layla, and Valdon Roosevelt, III. She is married to Valdon Roosevelt Daniel, II., from Athens, GA. They currently live in Scotch Plains, NJ.

I won't go as far as my dad and say everyone turned out perfect, but I think they did pretty well for themselves. Was it because of the spankings? Or, in spite of them? Hmm.

Chapter 12

THE SCRABBLE CLUB

A fter I retired from teaching, I was looking for something to do. I loved the game of "Scrabble" and was encouraged to start a club. It was the first Scrabble club in South Jersey, and I was the Director. We met at our church, Faith United Christian Church, in Berlin, NJ, a couple of times a month, which turned into once a week, because people kept coming. It was an incredibly fun, and popular game. We grew to almost 100 members and outgrew our own church. Walter's friend around the corner at the Berlin Baptist Church, Rev. Jerry Conover, allowed us to play at his church, and welcomed us with open arms.

The club continued to be active and even attended local and National Tournaments coast to coast, in various places around the country. These were fun to attend. We also gave local Tournaments ourselves. We joined the National Scrabble Association in New York, and they would send us games and prizes for our local Tournaments. Also, our local club took the game to area Nursing Homes and played with the residents there.

I trained some of the members to become Directors to help with the ever-growing club; some of them were: Herb Lewis, Marty Fialkow, Wayne Ollick, Lorraine Isherwood, and many others. One thing I liked about the club was that you got a chance to meet a wide variety of people. I used to tell people to join our club and meet the United Nations. There was no such thing as one size fits all. We had quite a variety. Some were tall and some were short, some skinny and some fat, some light and some dark, some jolly and some cranky; but we all had one thing in common…we all loved to play Scrabble.

The South Jersey Scrabble Club, Berlin, NJ

We have played in libraries, cafes in downtown Phila., Senior Centers, Churches, Fellowship Halls, and even in each other's homes. You name it; we played it. Most of us were retired, so it gave us something to look forward to doing, and it kept the brain active.

We also had annual picnics and cook-outs, and of course, played Scrabble. Members would bring a dish or their favorite dessert item, and we always had a festive time. One of our members, Greg McIntyre, would often invite us over to his mansion in Cherry Hill, and it was a treat to be served by his wife, Maggie, and the hired help. The local newspapers picked up on the evolving club; and ran several articles on us. This led to even more growth.

Life is always evolving. As we got older, more of us began playing Scrabble on our computers or smart phones. Many of us didn't drive at night anymore, so we stopped meeting on a regular basis. We did, however, continue to give Annual Tournaments, and to meet from time to time. It was a great outlet and fellowship. I made lifelong friends across the country, and some are still in touch to this day.

Chapter 13

STARTING A CHURCH

W alter started a Bible Study in our home in 1980, which led to the creation of the Sicklerville Christian Church in 1981. We worshipped in our house for almost a year before we outgrew it and moved to have our services at the Elementary School, (Number 3), here in Sicklerville.

**Sicklerville Christian Church at 11 Pinewood Lane
Sicklerville, NJ 08081**

Rev. Mc, as he was now being called, (and I was, Sis. Mc), were driving through Berlin, NJ, one day, and saw this lovely little church for sale. We thought it would be perfect for our congregation. It also had a 3-story building next door, whose downstairs was set up as a meeting or dining hall, complete with a kitchen and Pastor's Office.

We shared the good news with the congregation, and all agreed to move there. There was only one catch; actually, there were two catches. We didn't know the second catch, yet. The first one was that we had to come up with $10,000. dollars in 30 days, then we could go forward and assume the mortgage of the church that was leaving! Wow! Could it be done? We didn't know; we just stepped out on faith. We came up with the idea of selling "Bricks of Faith" for $10.00 each; and decided to see what would happen. We found favor with the Lord and others, and people came from all over to help us. Some bought 10 bricks of faith, and others bought as they were able. I remember my relatives in Oklahoma and California sending donations; also, churches, neighbors, relatives, and friends came forward and donated too. Praise the Lord. We made it!

Faith United Christian Church, Berlin, NJ
Founders: Rev. Walter & Betty McDaniel

Remember I told you about the second catch? Well, come to find out, we were on the wrong side of the tracks for a black church. The blacks were in the Township, and we were in the Borough. There was a great divide. We really hadn't thought about it or didn't even know, especially since the church we bought from was black. I say all this so you won't be as shocked as we were, when we tell you, that people smeared our church door with eggs, made us feel unwelcome, and ultimately threw a homemade bomb into the parsonage's window and injured one of our little children, David Crosby. You would think we were down South in 1919, not in 1985! What's wrong with people?

Courier-Post photo by Al Schell

Frank Crosby said his son, David, was 'really, really blessed' after being only slightly hurt in blast.

Pieces examined
from church blast

By KEVIN RIORDAN
Of the Courier-Post

BERLIN BOROUGH — Fragments of a projectile that broke through a window of a church-owned building, exploded, and slightly injured a 3-year-old boy were collected and examined yesterday by investigators from the Camden County Bomb Threat Task Force.

What those investigators are

describing as a "large bottle rocket" or "firecracker" apparently caused a small explosion at 8:20 p.m. Monday in a second-floor kitchen of a house next to the Faith United Christian Church, 117 Washington Ave.

The injured boy, David Crosby of Morgan Drive, Williamstown, was treated for a cut foot and released.

Please see BOMB, Page 6A

Newspaper Article on Church Bombing

I guess we are all victims of our times, and of what we have been taught or heard. One writer said that prejudice was ignorance. What do you mean by that, you might ask? It means to judge people (or things), simply by their appearance or how they look, and making assumptions about them, without getting to know them, or gather any facts. Let me give you some examples. Take flowers, for instance; some are red, some are yellow, some are white, etc. You can't say they are not flowers because their color is brighter or different than yours. No, they are all still flowers. Take the birds in the air. One breast is orange, and another is red. You cannot say one is not a bird because of its different color; or I'm better than you. Both are still birds. Take the fish in the sea. Some have stripes, some have dots, some are large, some are small. You can't judge them by looks; they are all still fish. God, in His infinite wisdom and creativity, gave us a variety of things; none better than others; none more precious than others...just physically different. He loves and respects all of His creation, and He expects you to do the same.

Apply this to people. We are all equal, and have the same value, in God's eyes. All have been marvelously and wonderfully made by their creator. Don't judge them. Learn them. Get to know them. Appreciate them, and their maker.

I also learned that prejudice was the actions of insecure people who needed something to look down on, so that they could feel better. What an awful waste of time and energy, not to mention the hurt and emotional damage it does to others. I like the way Dick Gregory put it. The question is not, why did you call me the "N" word; but the question is, why do you <u>need</u> the "N" word?

So, 'Hate Groups', you are out of line and lacking in understanding. Prejudiced people, you are missing the mark. To judge people because of looks, color, faith, or national origin, is sorely non-profitable, and it is against God; it's against people; and it's against your own well-being. Want to sleep well at night? Want to lose that frown and tangled up emotions? Want to know what pleases God and allows you to see peoples' worth? Seek your understanding and comfort in Him. Let Him have the control of your life. Relinquish your reigns to Him; follow His word; and watch how much better you will feel and act.

The recent Coronavirus, (COVID-19), reminds us that we are not in control. Any time a disease can jump over oceans, pass through lands, and eventually find you, tells you something. It doesn't care who you are, where you live, what race you are, what age you are, whether you're rich or poor, have health care or not, etc.; it found you. It is another reminder that we are all one, all the same, all of one blood, and all subject to the same diseases; and that God is in control!

Thank God for the scriptures that remind us that not only are we of one blood (Acts 17:26); but we are all equal in the eyes of God. He loves us all and we are made in His image. So, when you see people who are different than you, remember, they are made in God's image and He loves them all, and so should you.

Chapter 14
PREJUDICE, PART II

P rejudice can be so painful. I remember the time when
we were traveling home on the NJ Turnpike and stopped
at an exit for a bite to eat. The restaurant only had one long
counter open for patrons to eat. We followed the counter
around to the first empty seats, my husband and 3 small
children and myself. I did notice that the lights were a little
dim where we sat. At any event, we sat and sat, and watched
others get served except us.

Finally, a white man came in, and like us, saw there was
no seating except for the far end of the counter, and proceeded to sit on the other side of us. When I tell this story, I
like to relate that he barely sat his buns down on the stool,
when the white waitress ran over and told him not to sit
there because that section was closed! Needless to say, I
lost it! I went behind the counter and hawked that waitress
down and read her the riot act. "You saw my family sitting
here! Why didn't you tell us? If you can't waitress prop-
erly there are other jobs you can get, like house cleaning,
trash collecting, jobs not dealing with the public, etc., etc."
Meanwhile, Walter had found the manager and was giving
him an earful. The children just sat in stunned silence; and
waited for their parents to finish their tantrums.

I am happy to say that this was my last big public blow out with prejudice. I have since learned to be more sophisticated with my discontent: writing letters, making phone calls, contacting senators, etc. We like to say those were our B/C days, (Before Christ and Salvation). It was quite a challenge if you didn't know who you were in Christ, and that all people are created equal and have worth.

We were quite aware of the Civil Rights Movement at that time. Our whole thing was that the timing was off. We were trying to get through college; Walter was drafted into the military; we lived on base in Ft. Leonard Wood, MO; we returned to NJ and had to find employment; and we wanted to save and buy a house and start our family. We weren't able to participate in marches, or advocate for civil rights at this time. We just lived it; and corrected as we went! We also learned, later on, that the Lord had a different destiny for us to impact lives. It's called "Ministry work"!

I remember when my sister Doris and I went to hear Dr. Martin Luther King, Jr. speak in Philadelphia; he was so powerful and so good. We ran onto the stage when he finished; and wanted to shake his hand. His bodyguards staved us off about halfway on the stage. Dr. King motioned to them to allow us to come on. He accepted our hearty handshake as we told him how much we enjoyed his speech. My sister and I told our family and friends that we weren't going to wash our hands for a week, because we had shaken the hand of the great Dr. Martin Luther King, Jr.

We liked Dr. King, but we weren't in love with his approach to solving our problems. He was into passive resistance.

Coming out of the ghettos of South and North Philadelphia, we had no tolerance for people spitting on us, siccing dogs on us, or spraying us with hoses. Our first instinct was to fight back. On the other hand, the Black Panthers were too strong for me. They carried rifles and guns, and advocated freedom by whatever means necessary! Walter understood where they were coming from, but we just stuck to our goals and moved on. We did, however, join the protestors in their massive "March on Washington".

Finding our Roots and Moving on
Betty & Walter McDaniel

I read the autobiography of Malcolm X and was amazed and intrigued by it. It told how he evolved from being a man filled with hate, to a man with love and tolerance for all peoples. His trip to Mecca changed his whole life. When he returned to the States, he wanted to take America to the UN and to the World Court, for crimes against humanity (slavery). He was assassinated shortly thereafter.

We were also saddened by the death of other great leaders besides Dr. King. We were in Missouri when we learned of the death of John F. Kennedy. A woman ran out of her house crying and saying that they had just shot and killed the president. I really admired Pres. Kennedy; and was impressed with how he surrounded himself with the best minds of the country; and how he truly, wanted to make America better. His brother Bobby's murder also left a big hole in our hearts.

The biggest eye opener for me was to learn that <u>ALL</u> men came out of Africa. When we were kids, we didn't want anything to do with Africa, especially when they likened us to monkeys and apes, and being unattractive and having wooly hair. Come to find out, we <u>ALL</u> came from Africa and were only changed by climate, surroundings, diet, environment, etc. Check it out. There are plenty of history and historical books on this subject to enlighten you. If you don't know these things, you find yourself succumbing to the 'beat down' and feeling worthless and having low self-esteem. Thank God for my parents, my faith, my education, and my experiences.

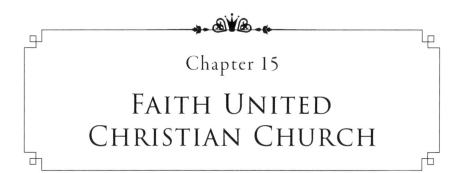

Chapter 15

FAITH UNITED CHRISTIAN CHURCH

B ack to our church in Berlin, NJ. Things quieted down for a while when they found out that we weren't going anywhere. We had to change the name of the church from Sicklerville Christian Church, since we were now in Berlin. Earline Williams, (who later became the Mother of the Church), came up with the name "Faith", saying, that's what it took to get the building. I came up with "United" because we all had to unite and come together to get the job done; and Walter wanted to remind everyone that we were a "Christian" church. My daughter, Linda, pulled it all together for us, and gave us, "Faith United Christian Church."

Despite our rocky start with the neighbors, the church took off and we have a lot of fond memories; and have blessed and educated a lot of people. We even wound up ministering to some of our neighbors who were formerly so hostile; and one in particular, who was now suffering from cancer. We had prayer with the cancer neighbor; and gave her hope, through the ministering of one of our members, Sis. Glenda Wrenn, who later became a minister herself.

Our children were also an integral part of the ministry since the very beginning. Paul became a Minister, Maria was church organist at one point, Linda sang a great alto, and evolved into our Worship Leader.

We settled in and began doing what churches do. We preached the word. We taught the word. We counseled people and couples. We built in fun events. We had our Annual Days: Men's Day, Women's Day, Founder's Day, etc. Every church has a Building Fund. We had a Children's Ministry and a group called "Teens for Christ". We had a standing annual program with Trinity AME Church in Bridgeton, NJ, and often brought in guest churches, choirs, and preachers.

Members

Members through the Years

Members through the Years

In the late 80's and early 90's, I started a Theater Ministry that traveled in and around NJ and other neighboring states. Our signature presentation was "God's Trombones", based on the writings of James Weldon Johnson. I turned it into a musical; and encouraged the churches where we performed to present it in a 'Dinner Theater' format. This went over well. Our choir would sing certain portions of the play, and other parts were read and/or acted out. This provided a great outlet for our young people and choir members, and we continued for quite some time.

THE SENIOR CHOIR—NELLIE JORDAN, ORGANIST

Organist Nellie Jordan

Sr. Choir Members

Jerry, Earline, Linda, Vivian, Betty, Dolly, Juanita

The Senior Choir—Nellie Jordan, Org.
Jerry, Earline, Linda, Vivian, Betty, Dolly. Juanita

SENIOR CHOIR–DONALD DRAFT, ORGANIST

Back Row: Earline, Shirley, Vivian
Front Row: Betty, Juanita, Dolly, Janie

Our church was always a little ahead of its time and encouraged Christian Rap when it first came out, and before it was fully embraced by other Christians. When our young members, John Wells and Cleveland Foat, first asked to perform, I remember telling John I had only one requirement... that they make the words plain and clear so that we could understand the message. Boy, did they ever. They went on to form a group called "The Cross Movement", that traveled locally and overseas, made records, won awards, performed before large crowds, and started their own recording studio.

I also remember encouraging my husband, Rev. Mc, when he first started preaching, to not only preach, but teach. In other words, don't just tell us what the Bible says to do and what not to do, but tell us how to do it! Give us scripture and examples of how to apply the word of God in our daily lives.

He took heed and wound up with a strong teaching ministry. It was through this ministry, taking classes and going to seminars, that I learned how to use and apply the word of God to my everyday living. It has blessed me ever since.

Throughout our ministry years, we 'adopted' some members and became Godparents to others: Georgia Harris; Patrice Dorell; David Crosby, Kevin Brown, Jr.; and Audrey Murray.

If I were asked what the highlight of our ministry was, I would have to say, training and preparing others to go into the Ministry and carry on God's work. Through the strong preaching and teaching of God's word, we were able to prepare and send forth over 20 ministers into the field of labor. Rev. personally trained and licensed 12: Frank Crosby, Kathleen Crosby, Paul McDaniel, Cleveland Foat, Kevin Brown, Sr., John Wells, Charles Miller, Darryl Farrar, Henry Hall, Donald Draft, Vernon Brown, and Paul Evans. Many of them started churches of their own, and the others got involved in: Youth Ministries, Music Ministries, Associate Ministers, Church Administrators, etc. To God be the glory!

Ministers trained and Licensed by Rev. McDaniel
Top: Cleveland Foat; Donald Draft; John Wells; Henry Hall
Middle: Paul McDaniel; Paul Evans; Frank Crosby; Kevin Brown
Bottom: Charles Miller; Darryl Farrar; Kathleen Crosby; Vernon Brown

Members who later became Pastors or Ministers
Top: Shirley Farrar; David Price; Glenda Wrenn
Middle: Yemi Koyejo; Demetrius Carolina; Allen Jenkins
Bottom: Karen Foote; Angela Brown; Toki Koyejo

After over 40 years in Ministry and Church Work, it was time to retire. I think we would have continued on, if Rev. hadn't gotten sick. Actually, what happened, was, he fell out of bed on two different occasions and hit his head (in the same spot, of course). He developed a large blood clot near the brain. They recommended surgery after doing several x-rays. They told him to get his house (and paperwork) in order, because there was no guarantee how he would come out afterwards. He might be the same; he might be partially the same; or he might not be the same with brain damage. What a blow! What a diagnosis! Reluctantly he called the family together and told them the grim news. He began establishing a power of attorney, a living will, trying to decide the fate of the church, etc. Needless to say, I was distraught and not of much help. However, we did have one tool left...Prayer. The saints began praying. Ministers prayed. Family prayed. We ran into a Bishop at a local restaurant and he laid hands on Rev. and prayed right there on the spot.

It was finally time to pack his little black bag and report back to the doctors to prepare for surgery. When we got there, the doctor said he wanted to take one more x-ray. When he returned to the room, his mouth was agape, and he was in shock! The large blot had dried up and there was only a thin line left; he couldn't believe it!

Rev. jumped up and gave him a bear hug. We all crowded around and did the same. We hoped we didn't embarrass the doctor, but this was too good of news to keep to ourselves. We ran out of there rejoicing and thanking the Lord!

Nevertheless, Rev. knew it was still time to retire. He was getting tired and realized he was not as sharp as he used to be. His preference was to turn the ministry over to one of his "Sons in the Lord"; however, they were all busy with churches or ministries of their own. He tried other ministers, but it just didn't seem to work out. He co-pastored with his assistant, Rev. Bette Carngbe until 2019. Her family has been a blessing to the ministry and a gift from God.

Deacon Peter & Rev. Bette Carngbe

Last Service at Faith United Christian Church
March 2019

Patience is a virtue. The Lord soon blessed us with a congregation that was looking for a church home. Their ministry was a perfect fit. Although we were sad to close this chapter of our lives, we were happy for them. We had so many precious memories, and so many had been taught and saved at the church. Where do you go from here? Do you ever really retire from doing the Lord's work? I don't think so. Rev. still counsels, buries, and teaches the saints; and is always available when he is needed or called. (And they still call...) He also teaches a Bible Study class at the VFW in Sicklerville, on Wednesday evenings, at 6:00 pm. Due to the recent Coronavirus, he now teaches the class virtually on Google Meet: same day, same time.

Retirement Banquet for Rev. McDaniel

Ministers & Wives gather around Rev. McDaniel at
Retirement Service at The Meeting House Church
Co-pastored by Darryl & Shirley Farrar

Chapter 16

LIFE AFTER RETIREMENT

Travel & The Sr. Citizens' Club

After Walter and I retired, we wanted to see the world before we got too old to travel and before the money ran out. We had Time Share, and we had traveled a bit with the kids, but now we wanted to travel more extensively; and, also, to take cruises. We visited all 50 states, and every island in the Caribbean. We took over 7 cruises. We also stayed several months during the winter, in Florida, visiting our son, Paul and his wife, and staying warm.

Some of our favorite trips were to: London-Paris-Rome; Hawaii; Alaska; Aruba; Bermuda; Jamaica. Our all-time favorite trip was the Mediterranean Cruise that took us to Egypt, Israel, Sorento, Greece and Italy. The camels and pyramids were awesome; not to mention the Holy Land encounter. We did a Dinner Cruise on the Nile River, and I couldn't help but think that this was the body of water that they slipped Moses into when he was a baby.

Our Panama Canal Cruise was awesome too. Sometimes we traveled alone, and sometimes we traveled with our good friends, Bill & Debbie Hicks, or Alvin & Roberta Stokes. All

in all, we felt very blessed to rise above our humble begin-
nings; and be able to travel around the world so extensively.

Places traveled: London, Paris, Alaska, Egypt

Some of our Memorable Trips

Another thing we wanted to do after we retired, was to
visit other churches. When you are in ministry work yourself, you don't have a lot of time to visit others. We made
it a point to visit our 'sons and daughters' in the ministry,
many of whom now had churches of their own. We also visited our families' churches, friends' churches, and churches
we were simply curious about. This was very enlightening
and a blessing, and we enjoyed it a great deal. Eventually,
however, we knew we had to settle down somewhere, and

decide on a church, and learn how to simply be a 'member' again. This was hard.

Our oldest daughter, Linda, had been attending Bethel Church in Blackwood, NJ, for a while, and encouraged us to attend. We found the people to be very friendly, engaging and sincere about their faith. Pastor Kurt Kinney, always brought the uncompromising word of God, and challenged your thinking. The church had Missionaries all over the globe, fed hundreds during the Thanksgiving holiday, had an annual "Week of Service" for those needing house repairs or services of any kind in depressed cities; and, actually lived out their faith. It was a multi-cultural church, and even offered headsets for those who spoke a different language. We were very impressed; and have been attending ever since.

When we weren't traveling, we thought we would look around and see what else retired seniors did. We made our way to the Winslow Township Senior Citizen's Club, in Atco, NJ. We had visited there before; but found out that there was only a small group of about 30 people who came out to play Bingo, went to the Casino monthly, and had Line Dancing. We thought we would check them out again and see if anything had changed. It had not.

As a matter of fact, it was during their time of election for President when we visited; and all we kept hearing from the crowd was, "I decline; I decline; I decline." I raised my hand and asked, "My goodness! What does the President do?" The outgoing President said, "Everything! Why? Do you want the job?" I told her I was just asking. Before I knew it, they ran over and gave me a set of keys; clapped and welcomed me aboard. I guess what they didn't know was, that if I really didn't want the job, or want to give it a try, that I would have surely spoken up. But something inside of me said that it might be a good challenge to get them to be more creative, and to bring in speakers and services for seniors, in addition to trips and outings. So, I told them that I would take the job; if they promised to help and support me.

You know how it goes. Some helped and some hindered. Some liked what I was doing, and some hated it. Some were encouraging and some were jealous. In the beginning it was hit and miss and learn through trial and error. After helping my husband run churches for over 40 years, it would take a lot to beat me down or run me out of the door. As they used to say at my church, "Take a licking and keep on ticking." And besides, I lived by my scriptures: (Colossians 3:23), says, "Whatever you do, do it heartily as unto the Lord and not unto men." Another scripture that inspired me was: (James 1:27), "Pure religion and undefiled before God is to visit the fatherless and widows in their affliction. I also kept the club in my prayers at night; so, I had my marching orders, plus I really wanted to see the Center succeed.

Another scripture that I saw fulfilled during this time was, (1 Chr. 16:22), "Touch not mine anointed, and do my prophets no harm." I saw several "Nay-sayers" go into the hospital, others move out of the state, and one, actually turned from being an enemy, to being a friend, and to being a helper! It was amazing to see God at work. Special thanks to Lucy Martelli who helped me early on, became a friend and mentor, and made my tenure more successful.

They had monthly meetings, so I started out by asking them what they wanted the Center to do. They mentioned: have a Newsletter, go on trips and outings, bring in speakers, and talk about senior information, and a host of other suggestions. I created an information form and asked for additional input and interests. I studied their ideas, carefully; and coupled them with my own personal thoughts; and began to put them into practice. The Newsletter was no problem, having been the Editor of my college newspaper.

Sample Newsletter from the Club

Also, having traveled the world, I could suggest a lot of trips. I loved the theater and plays; and wanted to bring them along with me. I thought they should also know about Medicare and retirement options and other senior information, so I brought in speakers and held seminars. Actually, this was a challenge for me, and allowed me to put into practice a lot of my life's experiences that I had learned.

Before we knew it, the club began to grow; so much so that I had to add a Board of Trustees to work along with me and the Officers. A couple of things I learned in life. The first thing is, that you can't do everything by yourself; you need help. Secondly, I learned that if you treat people with kindness and respect, they will respond positively towards you in return.

MY FIRST BOARD OF DIRECTORS

Back Row: Vi, Mary, Fran (Memb.), Lucy, Mayor Wright, Sonja, Evelyn, Marcia
Front Row: Terry (Sec.), Tina (VP), Betty (Pres.), Toni (Treas.)

I always had a heart for those less privileged or those whom the world called the 'underdog'; maybe because I was once considered one. I would take up for kids who were bullied or left out; intervene for adults who were too shy to speak up; stand up for minorities, etc. My seniors were no exception. I advocated for them whenever I could. They had already led a long and challenging life, and I felt that they should now enjoy their golden years. I used to tell them that I wanted their golden years to truly be 'golden'.

I began to take them on trips, to plays, and to the theater. We went to Phila. to hear the "Philly Pops" orchestra. We took train rides and bus trips to DC; Crab Feasts to MD; FL; outings to the Poconos in PA for weekly retreats, and took them on several cruises to Aruba, Panama, Canada, etc. We set up monthly payment plans that worked out well for them.

The Club continued to balloon, so much so, that we had to put a cap on membership. They were coming from all parts of New Jersey and even Pennsylvania. to join. So much for having a local Center! People from all over were clamoring to get in. We eventually had to limit membership to Winslow Township residents, only, which was the actual name of the Club. We went from 30 or so, members, to over 300! You talk about a success story! (See what prayer can do?)

I had a great Board of 10 that helped with the running of the Center. We organized, set up rules and procedures, listened to positive suggestions, weeded out the negative, met monthly to keep us on track; and stayed open to changes and improvements. Our motto was: if it worked, continue it; it if didn't work, pull the plug.

Another great plus was having the Mayor on our side. He too wanted us to succeed. He was always there with suggestions or help, listened to and acted upon our requests, provided us with things that we needed, from tables and chairs, to a new Bingo Board, to giving us sound advice.

My other big supporter was my husband, Walter. He not only drove me where I needed to go, or picked things up for me, or supported my events, but he was also there for me emotionally and spiritually; and he was always encouraging.

My next biggest supporter was Tina Spears, my Vice President. Tina was a 'Jack of all Trades', and we all called on her a lot. "Tina, the Bingo Board is not working; Tina, somebody spilled coffee on the floor; Tina, we're out of copy paper; Tina, Tina, Tina..." Most of the time she was a good sport about everything, although sometimes she would give you 'the eye', as if to say, 'What's wrong with you people?' All in all, she was a great help. She took a lot of little things off of me, so I could concentrate on bigger things, such as, getting speakers, meeting with the mayor or finance director, planning meetings, etc., etc.

Did I mention I went to FL for several months during our winters here in NJ? This meant that someone had to carry the torch while I was gone. Thank you for carrying on, Tina; and thanks to my Official Board: Tina, Terry, Toni, Fran, Vi, Sonja, Esther, Mary, Kathy, Dolores, Carmeta, and Gloria London, who is now the President. A shout out to Phyllis, who became my personal secretary, and helped me out a lot too.

Additionally, at the Center, we would: celebrate everyone's birthday, on a monthly basis, have meals on special occasions or holidays, send cards and updates to the sick, and make financial donations to families who lost loved one. We revised our By-laws to fit our current make-up. One of our main goals was to provide a safe and fun place for seniors to go.

We all looked forward to our annual "Christmas Party" and dressed up for the gala. We would have raffles, exchange gifts and cards, bring in entertainment, (such as the local high school choir, their Orchestra, the iDance Ministry, etc.). We would also hire a D/J; and dance the night away to the "Oldies". The Officers were recognized for their year of service, and the Mayor was always there for support and encouraging remarks.

We offered over 10 Programs and Outlets to the community at large, such as: Bingo, Tai Chi, Zumba, Movie & a Lunch, Line Dancing, Yoga, Bible Study, Food Give-away Program, Pinochle, Red Hat Club, Arts and Crafts, etc. You didn't have to be a member of the club to participate in these programs; they were free to anyone in the community.

Red Hat Club–'Sophisticated Seniors'
1st Row, 1st Person: Betty McDaniel, Founder
1st Row, 2nd Person: Sonja H. Bullock, Queen Mother

BOOK CLUB

Lexis, Joanne, Juanita, Linda, Rev. Bette, and me (Betty Carolyn)

We saw to it that they got the publication, 'The Senior Magazine' in addition to our Own Newsletter and Calendar each month. We brought in a variety of speakers: The Fire Marshall, the County Clerk's Office on Wills and Probates, Health Plans, and all sorts of things of interest to seniors. We had seminars on Diabetes, Balance and Wellness. We once had a speaker who came to show us how to claim any money that may be due us. Politicians were always in and out and leaving literature. Additionally, all members' trips were discounted, thanks to the Twp.

It was a great experience and a great time. Unfortunately, I got sick in 2018, after seven years of leadership, and had to step down. That was the bad news. The good news was that we had set up the Center with its programs and procedures so well, that they could still carry on. The other good news was that after over a year and a half, I had mostly recovered and was able to write this autobiography. I still attend the Center when I feel up to it, but I've had to cut back on trips and outings and involvements. God is still good, and I know I am a better person for the experience at the Winslow Township Senior Center. It brings me great joy to hear from the members; and how I impacted their lives. I was humbled and honored when they gave me a certificate of appreciation at our last Christmas party, presented by the Mayor. Early on, the local Business Association had given me a plaque for community service also. This too was greatly appreciated.

I had led a pretty healthy life for the most part. I never drank, or smoked, or did drugs. Eating habits were okay but could be improved. I still had my mental quickness, and seemingly an abundance of energy. I was still walking well and drove myself to most local places. I looked forward to traveling and attending events. All of this changed when I turned 80. It was almost as if life was saying, 'We're done here!' We celebrated my 80th birthday in January of 2018, and the next month, February, I was in the hospital. I woke up one morning and couldn't catch my breath. This led to a panic attack. And by the time the paramedics and ambulance came, my sugar was up, and my heart was beating rapidly. This led to a 4 day stay in the hospital. They discounted a stroke but wanted me to follow up with a cardiologist. This was the first of 4 hospital stays that year, and a 7 day stay at a Rehabilitation Center in Cherry Hill, NJ. I also spent 11 days at the MAYO Clinic in MN. I continued to have off and on breathing problems, but they couldn't seem to be able to put their finger on anything specific.

I was very tired, my balance was off, I had vertigo, double vision, and migraines. I had weakness in my hands and feet, and trouble concentrating and processing things. I went for test after test, to no avail. I was given a slew of pills and supplements. The best they could conclude was that this disorder was most likely from stress, and that I needed to rest and take it easy, and to continue to follow up with my doctors. Rest? There goes the Center... there goes running a church...there goes trips and outings... there goes family drama, and grandchildren interventions.

We were also displaced from our house because of a sewer pipe bursting on our property, and we were living in a hotel. My house was stripped bare, and they found asbestos under the floor. Walter was retiring from the church and was trying different ministers for his replacement. My daughter, Maria, was moving from VA back to NJ, and was staying with us during her transition. She came with a husband, 3 children and 2 dogs. Maybe I was a little stressed out after all.

Needless to say, I was not happy, nor was I feeling good; not to mention I missed being at the Center around my officers and friends, and the buzz and activity that took place. I felt I was behind in everything and letting people down. I had never been this sick before, and I felt sad and depressed. I couldn't drive or focus or sleep well at night. The migraine headaches didn't help either, something I had never had before. Thank God for His care, and my husband, and my daughter, Linda, and the prayers of the saints and family, that got me through those times.

I won't bore you with the gory details; let's just wrap this up with the fact that it took me almost two years before I began to feel more like myself. I'm still not a hundred percent, but I'm doing much better than before. I find I can't endure for a whole day, and sometimes I have to stop and rest. I'm only glad to still be here and functioning as best as I can. I miss being active and going to different places. I still try to hang in there with my "Book Club" buddies: Linda, Rev. Bette, Alexis, Juanita and Joanne; and participate in a few other activities, like the Red Hat Club; but I've learned to listen to my body and say 'no' when I have to.

They say dying is a part of the living experience, and no matter how many times you say to people, "I'm sorry for your loss", it only has real meaning when it involves you personally. The old folks used to say, "Thank, God, the family circle is still unbroken." I really didn't quite get it, until my mother died. I had been to aunts and uncles and grandparents' funerals, but a mother was a whole new ballgame, especially one who had been so loving and supportive through the years.

My mother had been in and out of hospitals for about 6 months. I was still working and running to the hospital when I got off. My older sisters were retired and were already there. Every time I got there, there was more bad news. I asked them, didn't they ever have any good news? They didn't. We had never had a close family death. Mother was only 72; so, when she died, I lost it. I had heard about a 'primal scream', but really didn't understand it until I reached down inside of me and found one! Did anyone really understand what I had lost? Only if you ever lost a really, close, dear one. The family called me, "Screaming Jay Hawkins", for a little while afterwards; I guess it was to lighten the pain.

Mother—Bettie Mary Douglas Isaac

My Dad cried for a solid year after her death; we weren't much better. There seemed to be a cloud of doom over us, every time we got together. I remember one day at church, we had a guest speaker, Rev. Jacocks, and she preached on trials and tribulations, pain and suffering. At the end of her sermon, she told the congregation to put their hand over wherever they were hurting, and she would pray for them. I put my hand on my heart. Vernon Brown was near me, and he grabbed his leg. Others indicated their pain also. After the service she came over to me and said that she saw a black cloud rise from me as she prayed, and how was I doing? Actually, I felt better, and I was able to complete the grieving process in peace from that day forward. My mother died in the hospital at 72. Dad died at 86, while pressing his way out to church. His companion said, while they were waiting for the bus (in Phila.), he kept saying, "I'm ready; I'm ready"; and then he collapsed to the ground. Here was a Legend gone; a Life well lived; a Longing to go home and be with the Lord and his loved ones. He was sorely missed.

Father–Homer Lee Isaac, Sr.

Walter's mother, Louise McDaniel, died at 86; His dad, Harry Lee McDaniel, Sr., died at 48.

Mother–Louise McDaniel

Father–Harry Lee McDaniel, Sr.
(God bless them both. They were a help and inspiration to us and our family.)

I used to hear the old folk talk about a 'Bucket List', back in the day. I didn't quite understand what they were talking about then; but I have come to understand it now. What they were saying, was, that there were certain desires or goals that they wanted fulfilled before they went on to 'glory'. This got me to thinking about my own 'Bucket List'. I came up with seven unfulfilled desires of my own: (1) A visit to Western Africa, our original homeland. (2) An opportunity to create or paint art professionally. (3) A desire to see my most creative play, "The Hot Seat", produced and brought to a theater. (4) To see my own children become settled and successful in their 'Life's Calling'. (5) See my grandchildren and great grands, continue the family tradition of education and a life dedicated to the Lord and others. (6) Live to settle all financial obligations, so I can leave my children an inheritance and not a debt. (7) And finally, leave room for the Holy Spirit, to lead and guide me to my 'Ultimate Goal' or calling in Christ Jesus.

I am writing this autobiography as a legacy for my children and grandchildren. I also hope that the extended family and others will get something out of it too. I want people to see that you can make it in life if you let the Lord lead you and guide you. Don't let others define you. Let God do it, and He already has. He tells you in His word that you are fearfully and wonderfully made, (Ps 139:14); and made in His image, (Gen. 1:27). The good news is that He loves you and wants the best for you. All He asks is that you keep His word and His commandments, and they are not grievous. He made you and knows what it takes for you to succeed while down here on earth.

I like the way He sums things up, "Love God and love your fellow man". You might ask, "How do you do that?" That's the problem. You can't. Only with the help of the Holy Spirit can you do it. Once you are saved, you are changed. The Holy Spirit comes and dwells within you and enables you to live a Godly life. How do you get saved? Go back and read my Chapter 9. There you will find all of the scriptures that you need to know, on how to get saved. They are found in the book of Romans, sometimes called "The Roman Road to Salvation". Get into a Bible believing church, attend regularly, attend Bible Study; ask questions, pray that the Lord will open up your understanding. Continue on, don't give up, persevere. Surround yourself with people who are 'going your way' so to speak. (II Cor. 6:14-18). Disentangle yourself from those going 'another way'. If you live long enough, you will see what their end will be, (Ecc. 8:13, and Psalm 1: 5-6). Start living the abundant life. Start following His word. Start putting joy back into your life. Love God and love others, and watch your life start to turn around. God makes a lot of promises to us: Healings, Prosperity, Protection from enemies, Long life, etc.; but they are only for the saved and those who walk in His ways. I'm sure you've tried all kinds of things to make life work, but to no avail. Now try God's way. I like the way the "Daily Bread" says it. "We all have a heart shaped vacuum in us, that can only be filled by God". Fill your vacuum with the word of God. Get yourself a good bible. But I can't understand the bible, you might say. Do you know there are two things that can help you with this?...the Holy Spirit, and the many versions of the bible, such as: The NIV, NKJ, ASV, RSV, CSB, BRG, CEV, ESV, and the Reader's Digest Version. When I was a new Christian, my all-time favorite was, The Good News Bible. It was written in plain English and it had pictures!

We always enjoyed reading different versions of the bible from cover to cover. Just remember, the bible is not a smorgasbord, where you get to pick and choose what you want to believe; or take away only what suits you. You must eat the 'whole' thing. Every word of God is true, and He put certain things in it because He knew that they would help you to overcome; and lead a successful life. He is our maker. Trust me; He knows what is best!

May God bless you and keep you as you start your own journey through life. Live it well. Try a variety of good things. Don't be afraid to learn from others, especially those who have lived a successful life. Read a variety of books. Never get stuck on just one way of thinking or doing things. And above all, learn to forgive and love people, and remember that we are all human.

Chapter 17

THE 50TH WEDDING ANNIVERSARY

O n another note, I forgot to mention that around 2008-
2009, going on our 50th Wedding Anniversary, I got
this bright idea that I wanted another formal wedding to
renew our vows. Actually, it wasn't my own bright idea. My
parents had celebrated their 50th Anniversary with a wedding
renewal service, with the colors white and gold. I thought it
was really, breathtaking, and promised myself that I would
do the same, if I made 50 years. My siblings, and I, were in
our parent's 50th celebration, along with our spouses. Family
and friends came from all over to help them celebrate, and
it was a very special event.

Fast forward to our 50th anniversary in 2010. I knew it
was going to take some planning if we were going to pull
this off, thus I needed one or two years prior to plan it. I
decided to use my own children in the wedding, and their
first cousins. They would need time to pay for their gowns
and suits, and to make any arrangements.

Since I was doing a complete wedding, it did take the
entire 2 years to plan. Some of the cousins were in Detroit,
Connecticut, Pennsylvania, and different parts of New Jersey.

I had 3 grandchildren at the time who would be perfect for 2 flower girls, and the boy for the ring-bearer. Our church was not big enough, so we opted to use the Lutheran church around the corner. Invitations had to be sent, a place for the reception acquired, my gold gown located, and not to mention, convincing the cousins to participate. Our good friend, Rev. Alvin Stokes, agreed to perform the ceremony, and another good friend, Rev. Paul Evans, agreed to walk me down the aisle.

Walter & Betty McDaniel—Renewing 50th Wedding Vows

It was a lot of fun but a lot of work. Event planning, I thought, was one of my strong points, so I dived in and began the process. Oh, did I mention we needed a photographer? And what about the music? I wanted "Ave Maria" sung, the same song from our original wedding; and Stevie Wonder's, "Isn't She Lovely" for our exit song. The event was getting larger than life. Did I get in over my head; with 7 bridesmaids and 7 groomsmen? I won't say things went off without a hitch; but we eventually pulled it off. The hardest part was finding a gold veil or head piece. We wound up dying a white one gold. Did we want a limo? No! Just get in cars and drive around to the reception. Did you ever want something to just be over? I think that was the case here.

The Bridal Party: Keysha Isaac, Kimberly Parks, Diane McDaniel, Lenee Bernard, Maria Daniel, Carolyn Hart, Linda Gathie, Walter McDaniel Betty McDaniel, Paul McDaniel, Doug Gathie, Homer Isaac, III, Warren McDaniel, David Price, Valdou Daniel, II, Melvin Rowden, Aliyah Daniel, Amanda Daniel, & Valdou Daniel, III

The Complete Wedding Party

We received lots of nice presents and cards. My daughters, Linda and Maria, saw to it that we received tributes from many of our political leaders: President Obama, Governor Christie, Senator Menendez, Senator Lautenberg, Representative Andrews, and Winslow Twp. Mayor Metzner.

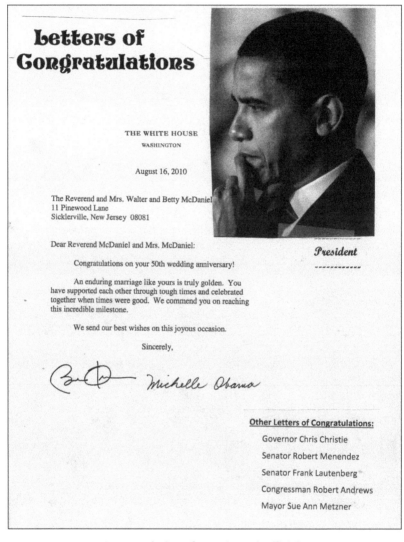

Letters of Congratulations

THE WHITE HOUSE
WASHINGTON

August 16, 2010

The Reverend and Mrs. Walter and Betty McDaniel
11 Pinewood Lane
Sicklerville, New Jersey 08081

Dear Reverend McDaniel and Mrs. McDaniel:

Congratulations on your 50th wedding anniversary!

An enduring marriage like yours is truly golden. You have supported each other through tough times and celebrated together when times were good. We commend you on reaching this incredible milestone.

We send our best wishes on this joyous occasion.

Sincerely,

Michelle Obama

President

Other Letters of Congratulations:
Governor Chris Christie
Senator Robert Menendez
Senator Frank Lautenberg
Congressman Robert Andrews
Mayor Sue Ann Metzner

Congratulations from Elected Officials

Everyone enjoyed themselves and we had a festive time; but I looked forward to crawling into bed that night. Oh, I forgot. There would be no crawling into bed. We had to head out for our "Honeymoon" to Niagara Falls, on the Canada side! All in all, it was a spectacular event, and the album came out lovely. The only thing I forgot was that getting married and planning a wedding at 22, was much different than planning a wedding at 72!

We recently celebrated our 60th Wedding Anniversary (8/27/20). We knew we couldn't have a large event or gathering, because of the Coronavirus, so we opted instead to have a 'Drive-by Shout Out'. We encouraged everyone to drive by, blow their horn, and/or leave a card in the mailbox if they chose; while we waved and greeted them from the porch.

Well, wouldn't you know it; it rained like cats and dogs that day! We just knew no one was coming in this bad weather; the balloons were withering, the grass was wet, and the day was cloudy. We concluded that Satan was furious; and wanted the event to flop. How dare a couple put on display the fact that the Lord kept them together for 60 years! Some people don't stay together for 60 days, let alone 60 years! How can we sabotage this event?

But low and behold, they did come. The Mayor came first; and handed us a Proclamation. This was followed by family and friends, coming from: Willingboro, Delaware, Westhampton, Mt. Laurel, Scotch Plains, Phila., and surrounding neighborhoods, etc. We were amazed! One couple came twice, having come previously on the wrong day. Others came later after the rain downpour ceased, and a few, drove by that night. The absentees, sent texts, and cards, and that was appreciated too. They came to pay tribute to us; but for us, the tribute should go to them, for pressing out, on such an ungodly day!

Chapter 18

FINAL CONCLUSIONS

L et's wrap this up and leave you with some food for thought. As King Solomon said in (Ecclesiastes 12:13), "Let us hear the conclusion of the whole matter. Fear God and keep His commandments. For this is the whole duty of man."

I don't know if you noticed that throughout my whole autobiography, there was a lot of emphasis on scripture or doing things God's way. That is because I have learned that is what makes life work.

You might read and simply conclude that we lived a great, trouble free life. Not so. We had our ups and downs and hard times, just like the next fellow. In marriage, we argued, fought, disagreed, separated, like any other couple. You can't live with another person 24/7 and not have altercations. Remember what scripture says in (Gen. 6:5), "...every imagination of the thoughts of man are only evil, continuously"; and (Proverbs 16:2) says, "All the ways of a man are clean in his own eyes". So, you see, we start out handicapped, and think we are always right!

Well, what made it work for you, you might ask? The minute we were saved. The minute we committed to doing things God's way. The minute we got away from putting "I" first. The minute we decided to work together rather than argue together. The minute we decided to care for each other above ourselves. The minute we learned what the scriptures said about marriage, covenants, commitments, and communications. Believe me, it wasn't easy, and it took some time. But by allowing the Holy Spirit to work in us, guide us and teach us, we were well on our way. Voices were lowered; "Life is all about me", was diminished; Fruit of the Spirit began to develop (Gal. 5:22-23), and we began to look more like God's children. We continued to fall and stumble at times, but not as easily, and not as often. We continued to grow.

My advice to others, let go and truly let God. Yes, some people move along and appear to be making it without God; but if you really want to make it and lead a rich and successful life, live it God's way. The Bible is not a big, old, dusty book full of do's and don'ts, but a guide for living well and abundantly while here on earth. Just think. God made you; and He knows what it will take to survive and live victoriously while down here on earth.

I have lived life B/C (Before I accepted Christ); and A/C (After I accepted Christ). Trust me. A/C is the best way, and only way, to make life work successfully for you.

If someone were to ask me, what are the most important things you have learned in life, in your 82 years here on earth, I would have to tell them, these concepts:

1–**There is a God!** He made everything. He made you. ALL people are human, and ALL are equal. ALL were made by the same creator and are 100% alike. Some may be taller or shorter, lighter or darker, fatter or thinner... but they are ALL alike! ALL have hearts, livers, kidneys, lungs, etc., ALL are alike. ALL have gifts, talents, and abilities, ALL alike. ALL have been made by God. ALL are precious in His sight!

2–**Life is not all about you!** Life is about **LOVE**: Loving God, loving others, and then loving yourself. We were always taught to look out for No. 1, yourself. No! You have to flip the script; you have to love others, first. Do for them. Help them. Have compassion for them; then all good things will come back to you. You will have fulfilled the Great Commandment: (Mat. 22:36-40). You will have done what is required of you. You will be at peace with your Maker, and with yourself, and you will lead a joyful and successful life.

3–**Embrace Change!** Life is always evolving. Don't get stuck in the past, or continue to do things the old way, if times have changed. Case in point. We used to have volumes and volumes of information in encyclopedias. Now all you have to do, today is, "Google it". Move along with the times and stay current. Life is full of new and expanding experiences. Grab them! Regardless of your age, your circumstances, your condition, or your past...keep learning, keep growing, keep moving on, and embrace life's changes.

4–<u>Dealing with Trouble and Hard Times!</u> Life is a series of trials and tribulations. As a matter of fact, it seems as if they are stacked up at the door, waiting for one trial to finish, so another one can come in. You have two ways to respond: (1) Like the world does–fuss, cry, lament, whine, why me? or... (2) You can respond the way the Lord tells us to; and also learn <u>why</u> we have to go through these things. (Heb. 12:3-13; Jam. 1:2-4; 1 Pet. 4:12-19.) I also found out that in every trying situation... there is a lesson to be learned. (God does not waste our pain.) Be sure to get the message that comes with your trials and tribulations, even if it's just simply to learn how to wait, trust, and obey. Sometimes God is busy working things out for you. Sometimes life is about the timing. Also, sometimes there are hard lessons in life that you need to learn, that can only be learned through certain trying and painful situations.

5–<u>Always Tell the Truth!</u> Even if it's a hard truth. Always be honest with people. The key is <u>how</u> you tell people. If you're going to point your finger at them, and roll your neck, it's not going to work. But if you gently approach people, and say what you have to say in <u>love,</u> then you are well on your way. It also helps to point to yourself first, such as: When I was your age...; I remember when...; What I have learned in such a situation...etc., etc. Also, look for 'Teachable Moments'; (many times after a catastrophe); these are times when a word from the wise is proper and fitting, and the hearer is ready to receive it. And above all, remember what the Daily Bread says, "When you walk in integrity, you never have to look over your shoulder!" (Also read about Godly Communications in Eph. 4:29-32).

Chapter 19

TIMELINE OF EVENTS

1938–Born in Oklahoma City, OK, Jan. 22

1940–Family moved to Philadelphia, PA

1941–Moved to 1309 S. Napa Street, in South Phila.

1941–Started kindergarten at James Alcorn Elementary School

1940's and 1950's–Grew up on Napa Street in South Phila.

1949–Graduated from Alcorn Elementary School; moved on to Audenried Jr. High School

1952–Graduated from Audenried; moved on to West Phila. High School

1955–Graduated from West Philadelphia High School

1955–1957–Worked for the City of Phila., and the Phila. Navy Yard

1958–Started Cheyney State Teachers College

1958–Selected to be the Freshmen Homecoming Queen

1959–Became engaged to Walter A. McDaniel

1960–Married Walter A. McDaniel, 8/27/60

1961–Walter graduated from Cheyney, started teaching at Stanton Elementary School, Phila.

1962–I graduated from Cheyney and started teaching at Tildon Jr. High School in Phila.

1962–Walter was drafted into the US Army

1963–I joined Walter at Ft. Leonard Wood, MO, and taught at elementary school on the Base

1964–Returned to Phila. and began teaching at Shoemaker Jr. High School

1965–Bought our first home in the Mt. Airy section of Phila.

1966–Traveled with the Methodian Concert Choir cross-country: to OK, UT, NV, CA

1966–Started the Las Damas Lady's Club in Phila,

1967–First child born, Linda Louise McDaniel,

1968–Taught night school at Gratz High School in Phila.

1969–Son born, Paul Walter Lee McDaniel,

1970–Taught Adult Basic Education in Phila.

1971–Second daughter born, Maria Antoinette McDaniel

1972–Moved to Los Angeles, CA; stayed with Grandmother, Helena Williamson

1973–Taught Jr. High School in L.A., and sold jewelry for Celebrity Fashion Jewels

1974–Moved to Morganton, NC. Taught at elementary school there

1975–Moved to Whiteville, NC–Taught reading for 2 years in Tabor City, NC School

1976–Organized the "Third World" choir in Whiteville, NC

1977–Moved to Powder Mill Springs in Mays Landing, NJ; taught Adult Basic Ed. in AC

1978–Began teaching at Oakcrest High School

1979–Moved to Sicklerville, NJ

1980–Betty had major surgery at Virtua Hospital in Voorhees, NJ

1981–Started the Sicklerville Christian Church at the house

1982–Walter left the AME's

1983–Transferred to Egg Harbor Twp. High School

1984–Homer & Bettie Isaac's 50th Wedding Anniversary Celebration

1985–Walter & Betty McDaniel's 25th Wedding Anniversary

1985–Bought Faith United Christian Church in Berlin, NJ

1986–Linda graduated from Edgewood High School, NJ, and went to Norfolk State, VA

1987–Paul graduated from Edgewood and went to Camden County College, NJ

1988–Maria graduated from Edgewood and went to Spelman College in Atlanta, GA

1989–Took Theater Ministry on the road, presenting our version of "God's Trombones"

1990–Mother died, Bettie Mary Douglas Isaac

1991–Had complete physical collapse at Egg Harbor Twp. High School

1992–Officially retired from teaching after 30 years

1993–Maria was crowned "Miss Black Minnesota"; I started the SJ Scrabble Club of Berlin

1994–Linda graduated Suma Cum Laude from the University of MN

1995–Paul married Sherry Buckmon

1996–First grandchild born, Imani McDaniel

1997–Walter and I traveled to Aruba, Puerto Rico, and Hawaii

1998–Maria graduated from Rutgers School of Law

1999–Maria married Valdon Roosevelt Daniel, II

2000–Mama died, Louise McDaniel; Linda got Doctorate from University of VA

2001–Dad died, Homer Lee Isaac, Sr.; 2nd grand born, Aliyah; Paul married Diane Mmari

2002–Linda married George Cathie, Jr. (Doug)

2003–3rd grand born, Valdon R. Daniel, III

2004–Phyllis Rowden died; Aunt Leora died

2005–4th grand born, Ananda L. Daniel; 50th Reunion, West Phila. High; Alaska Cruise

2006–Isaac Family Reunion in Phila; Walter retired from Winslow Twp. Middle School

2007–Went to Rick Warren's seminar on "40 Days of Purpose" in Calif.

2008–Celebrated my 70th Birthday

2009–Walter in hospital for heart stints

2010–Went to Anguilla for Brenda Isaac's 50th Birthday; Celebrated our 50th Wedding Annv.

2010–Grands, Aliyah, Valdon & Ananda, all came up for salvation at Faith United Church

2011–Paul and Diane moved to FL; Aunt Enola Cummings died

2011–I became President of the Winslow Twp. Sr. Citizens' Club, Atco, NJ

2012–Best cruise ever to Mediterranean: Rome, Egypt, Israel, Greece, Sorento

2013–Paved and striped parking lot at Faith United

2014–Died: Carolyn Hart and Verolga Nix

2015–Doug Cathie had horrific car accident, needed jaws of life & air lift

2016–Walter retired from the ministry

2017–Sewer pipe burst; lived in hotel for 2 months; Maria moved back to NJ from VA

2018–I got sick. In and out of 4 hospitals, One Rehab, and MAYO clinic for 11 days in MN

2019–Retired as Pres. of Sr. Center; Mother Earline died.

2020–Walter's 80th; Our 60th Annv.; Rev. Stokes died; Coronavirus ravished the entire world!

2020–George Floyd was murdered by police, and there were demonstrations in US and abroad!

Sometimes, it's hard to remember everything you've read; therefore, I'll leave you with the
"5 Main Points to lead a Successful Life":

1. **FAITH:** Find your faith and live it. Share it; and grow with others. Learn how to apply the Word of God to everyday circumstances, and walk in your faith.
2. **EDUCATION:** Whether it's: college, computer classes, reading a variety or multitude of books, or Bible Studies— you need to know and be informed. You need to grow in your faith, life, and understanding.
3. **PEOPLE:** We are ALL of the same blood, equal, and made by the Father. We should, love, learn and fellowship with one another. Surround yourself with Godly people who are living Godly lives.
4. **DETERMINATION:** Let nothing or anyone turn you away from your Goals, or living a Godly life. Disentangle your-self from people who are not going your way. Press on. Stay focused. Persist to the end.
5. **GIFTS**: The Lord has given you certain gifts and talents. Discover them. Use them for the glory of God and to bless other people.

Can't remember all 5? Memorize and walk in this
One Scripture:
(Luke 12:29-31). Look it up. It says it all.

Blessings upon you as you start your own successful journey through life.

MY WRITINGS

By: Betty Carolyn Isaac McDaniel

Chapter 20

ORIGINAL WRITINGS BY THE AUTHOR

I. POEMS -
1. Rain
2. Asleep in the Hammock
3. Grandchildren
4. Teens
5. My Neighborhood
6. Father was Tired
7. Ancestors
8. A Martian's Take on Mother's Day
9. The Oddest Story (About Jesus)
10. Tis the Season
11. I Came to the Lord
12. For the New Year
13. When a Prayer Isn't Answered
14. The Answer Has Come
15. Rhythm of the Sea

II. SKITS -
1. The Real Meaning of Easter
2. The Story of Jesus

III. PLAYS -
1. Angel Eyes
2. The Hot Seat (This Play includes two Musical Scores)

MY POEMS

RAIN

Pitter, patter, hear the rain
Pat, pat, patting on my windowpane
Go away, oh can't you see
All my friends want to play with me.

Pitter, patter, hear the rain
Pat, pat, patting on my windowpane
Go away, oh can't you see
All the mud will splash over me.

Pitter, patter, hear the rain
Pat, pat, patting on my windowpane
Go away, oh can't you see
Puppy is as wet as he can be.

ASLEEP IN THE HAMMOCK

He lay there snoring, oblivious of the day
Nocturnally ignoring, the scenes that passed his way

A fly came calling; he twitched it with his nose
A bee came falling, at this he almost rose

A fire engine clanged; his ears seemed to do a flip
An airplane took to the sky; he merely curled his lip

It then began to rain, and soaked him through and through
He wasn't trying to feign it; he slept right through that too

Now for the impossible fable, mother called to him with care
Dinner is on the table; he jumped straight in the air!

GRANDCHILDREN

Grands, grands, grands,
boy are they ever fun
If it were left up to them,
they'd play all day in the sun

They come with bounteous energy,
from morning until night
And as far as the little ones go,
better not let them out of your sight

Mom-Mom, let's do this,
and Pop-Pop let's do that
Can we bake cake and cookies?
they ask with a loving pat

Here's a little candy,
don't let your mother see
You know how she is about sweets
she'll blame your bad teeth on me

I want to stay with Mom-Mom,
she's very nice and fun
And Pop-Pop let's us play,
even after the day is done

The parents shake their heads,
it's a mystery what they see
They can't believe their own parents,
are now what they've come to be

What is wrong with this here picture?
they never treated us so kind
They made us tow the mark,
and you always had better mind

Are they now old and addled brain?
They have surely lost their wits
Or are they now two "fuddy duddies",
trying to get into heaven and fit?

The grandparents continue without notice,
it's as if they were given another chance
To love these sweet angelic beings,
who make their life so enhanced

As one grandmother said with a smile,
I'm not saying my kids were the worst
But if I could have had my "druthers",
I would have had my grandchildren first!

TEENS

Teenagers have been placed here on earth
To test our very metal
To try to give them sound, answers
On this they will not settle

They're bent on doing things their way
They know it all, and they feel grown
If you try to introduce something new
They'll grouch and say, Leave me alone!

Why don't you buy this lovely dress?
It's a pretty shade of red.
No, she grimaces. I don't like it
I'll take this black one instead

Son, isn't it time you got a job?
You've been out of school for a year
Who's rushing me, and on my case
I'll get a job, you hear?

I like the way one parent said
Put them in office in City Hall
Then let them run the government
While they still know it all!

MY NEIGHBORHOOD

Now I grew up on a very small street,
there were plenty of people that you could meet
All ages, all sizes, we had them all,
so, if you wanted company, all you had to do was call

We lived in row houses, side by side,
they were narrow and small, and not very wide
The houses were built for just a few,
but most were packed, what could you do?

But the play and fun outweighed it all,
we had lots we could do, whether spring or fall
Everyone loved to have a good time or two,
there was always something fun waiting for you

The neighbors all kept an eye on you,
and didn't mind telling all that you would do
You see, back then, we were "One Big Family",
whatever you did, everyone could see

Nevertheless, we wouldn't have changed a thing,
all added their own touch of things to bring
If you called your uncle, "Uncle Joe Brown",
so did everyone else who lived in the town

We all walked to school, there was no bus,
we didn't even think, to make a fuss
Children gabbed and played all the way to school,
eager to learn that golden rule

There were shops and stores on all the main streets,
you could always go to one and buy a treat
A penny went a long way, back in the day,
you took it gladly and went on your way

Soda bottles were redeemed for a penny or two,
that was a great way to make some cash for you
Don't forget the salvage place down the street,
you saved those papers and didn't leave a sheet

After dinner we played a lot of games,
from Dodge Ball to Baseball, all you could name
'Course when it got dark, you had to go inside,
sometimes Dad would take us for a ride

Saturday meant get up and start to clean,
wash clothes and dust, whatever was seen
If you did all your chores and finished in time,
you could go to the movies for only a dime

We never even knew that we were poor,
although sometimes we wished for more
But since everyone else was in the same boat,
there was no need to sit around and mope

They say time flies when you're having fun,
telling stories and jokes when day was done
We just lived each day to the very "max",
those were great times, and that's a fact.

FATHER WAS TIRED

The door slammed with a bang, and Father came in
You could tell by the sound, just where he had been
Working his shift at the company warehouse
His boss was mean, a real true louse
So, stay out of his way and don't fool around
Best you tip and be quiet and try not to be found
Father was tired
He woofed down his meal and grunted at the cook
She fed him some more without even a look
After his meal he checked out the mail
More bills and more threats, the same old tale
He tore them to shreds and hurled them right out
You knew he was mad; he didn't have to shout
Father was tired
He laid on the couch to take a nap
Before he shut an eye, there came a rap
A boy looking for Chucky to play some ball
Dad frowned as he motioned him down the hall
Maybe a little TV would hit the spot
But then he remembered the tubes were out
Father was tired
He put on his hat and went for a walk
Maybe he'd find old Dave, and they could talk
On his way, he stumbled up on a drunk
Further down the street, he had to circle some junk
Two ruffians came along looking for someone to try
One look at Dad and they quickly passed him by

Father was tired
When he got to the Center, old Dave was there
He motioned him over, and Dad took a chair
"Sit down, dummy, let me teach you to play"
That's all Dad needed to hear him say
He slapped those checkers around and HE was the boss
Dave didn't stand a chance, he chalked up the loss
Father was tired!

ANCESTORS

Now this story is true, I really swear to you
I couldn't have made it up, even if I wanted to
Now a certain young man (I won't mention his name)
Wanted to know all his history, and from whence he came
He swabbed both cheeks, and sent his DNA away
Let's just see what these experts now have to say
As he waited and waited, visions raced in his head
He wondered what tribe he was, and what people
they'd lead
He was sharp as a tack, and up on his history
He knew he came from Africa, that was no mystery
Perhaps the Song High Empire, was from where he came
Or the Sutus or Bantus, or other tribes he could name
Time passed very slowly, and he really wanted to know
Every day he checked the mailbox,
down the walkway he would go
People asked him about the cost,
he said he didn't mind the fee
Money was no object, if he could trace his history
Now you have to understand, the importance of this cause
We were denied our history, they even passed laws
Well, finally the results came one evening in the mail
He leaped into the air, and hoped his heart wouldn't fail
He tore that envelope open, and couldn't wait to see
His ancestors, his history, what tribe would he be?
But suddenly a shock came all over his face
Was it bad? Was it good? Was it even a disgrace?

Come on and share with us, tell us, did you get your wish?
The poor man's DNA said, he was definitely, IRISH!

A MARTIAN'S TAKE ON MOTHERS' DAY

A Martian once came to earth to see
Just what all the fuss about Motherhood could be
So, he looked high and low, and from East to West
He could see Mothers struggling and giving their best
From early in the morning, 'til late at night
They were teaching and training children to do
what was right
Cooking and ironing and washing and mending
Shopping and marketing and carefully spending
Some could be seen minding children and tots
Others could be seen with a different type of lot
Molding teenagers to best cope with strife
Or sending young adults out to wrestle with life
But don't think for a minute that this was the end
For they came back to Mother with babies to tend
And it seemed like the cycle started over again
Leaving one wondering, where is the end?
So, the poor confused Martian departed on his way
And when asked about Motherhood, he had this to say
Well, it's a lifetime job, 24 hours a day
And once every year, they let her have her way.

THE ODDEST STORY
(About Jesus)

The children all looked at me in awe
They couldn't believe the thing they saw
I showed them a book about Jesus, the baby
They asked was it real or simply a maybe?
Where is Santa, and who is this child?
They'd never heard of anything so wild
Christmas is all about presents and toys
Dolls for the girls and trains for the boys
This babe in a manger is something new
Are you sure this story is even true?
What does it mean and why don't we know
If this is the truth, then tell us so
Tell everyone young and everyone old
They themselves must not, have ever been told
Does this story mean we won't have any fun?
Or get toys and gifts when the day is done?
This Christ you say was born today
And he's the reason and only way
And we should all learn more about him
Not look about but look within
It's nice to get and give to others
We're all one people, all sisters and brothers
But remember whose day it really is
And emphasize Christ, the day is His!

TIS THE SEASON

Oh, tis the season, shining bright
Amidst the cold and dim sunlight
What is that star? What does this mean?
It speaks of things as yet unseen
Oh, tis the season, shining bright
Amidst the cold and dim sunlight
Although unseen we know the tale
Just read your Bible, it won't fail
Oh, tis the season shining bright
Amidst the cold and dim sunlight
It tells of God's miraculous birth
It tells us how He came to earth
Oh, tis the season shining bright
Amidst the cold and dim sunlight
He is the one from high above
Who came to tell us we are loved
Oh, tis the season shining bright
Amidst the cold and dim sunlight
He let's us know we need not fear
When life is over, He'll be so near
Oh, tis the season shining bright
Amidst the cold and dim sunlight
There'll be no cares, or struggles, or sin
He'll take us all home, to live with Him!

I CAME TO THE LORD

I came to the Lord, just as I was
Broken into a thousand pieces
He took me right in
Forgave all my sin
And lead me to all that He teaches
I came to the Lord, just as I was
Bowed down and filled with shame
It mattered not to Him
He saved me right then
A new soul He reached down to claim
I came to the Lord, just as I was
He forgave me and made me His own
My burdens became lighter
My outlook was brighter
My life took a whole new tone
I came to the Lord, just as I was
He told me to go and tell others
How He was the way
He'll save you today
We will all become sisters and brothers

FOR THE NEW YEAR

Twelve more months have come and gone
They really whizzed by and didn't take long
What are your thoughts on this year that has passed?
It really went its way, very, very fast
I'm sure there were things you wanted to do
But left undone because for you
There were people to meet, and places to be
There were dates to keep and things to see
Your list of "To Do" was getting long
How did that happen, and what went wrong?
You can't turn the hands of the clock back now
It's an impossibility, and we don't know how
So that was last year and this one is new
Let's see if there're ways that we can do
Things bigger and better than last year's try
Different and new; let's reach for the sky!
Step boldly and bravely into this year
Do not look back and have no fear
You're given another chance to do
All of those things confronting you
Be steadfast and true and go your own way
Fulfil all your dreams and tasks today
So when 12 more months roll around again
There will be no doubt; you will surely win

WHEN A PRAYER ISN'T ANSWERED

Night and day, you sent prayers up,
expecting answers soon
But echoes came back emptily,
singing a different tune
Why, oh why, has no answer come,
I prayed within His grace
Must I be tormented and left unfilled,
until I see His Face?
We want an answer to our prayers,
the Good Book tells us so
If we abide within His grace,
He'll answer and let us know
But days go by, and even years,
and no answer seems to come
Perhaps He didn't hear me then,
or know where I was coming from
I'll try again and this time be,
more specific and much more clear
I know He'll hear me at this time,
and answer and draw me near
But, again, there's silence, and no answer,
I'm beginning to lose all hope
It's maddening and discouraging;
I feel let down; how will I ever cope?
And just as I was about to give up,
and decided no answer would come

A still, small voice, spoke to my soul,
and said, Come, child, and listen some
Remember God answers all your prayers,
with one of three replies
Yes, or no, or wait awhile,
on this you can rely
God is not interested in a speedy,
swift answer, to any of your prayers
He is more interested in your heart
when you lay your burdens there
Do you really want a Godly answer,
or is it all about you?
Hurry up Lord, and ease my pain,
I know what you can do
But remember, no meat was ever done,
with a quick fire, and instant flame
It had to stay and slowly cook,
and so you must do the same
Therefore, let God keep working on your heart,
He knows just what you need
Keep sending those prayers right on up to Him,
In His time, He will surely heed!

THE ANSWER HAS COME

The answer has come, after years of pining... whining
Dare I hope again? Can I now believe... conceive?
All hope was gone, I was slowly sinking... shrinking
But now you say, I can smile... awhile?
Lift my head up high, give a shout... not a pout?
Such a long time has passed, I lost my zeal... appeal
If I step out on faith, once again...and don't sin
Will I get burned, once more...as before?
I'm spiritually spent, my soul is lean...and unseen
I tried my best, I did the good...as I should
I never held back, I gave my all...and walked tall
It's hard to look up, when you've been down...
to the ground
If I look up, will the tears flow...as I go?
Will I be set up, once more...as before?
Oh, mustard seed of faith, take heart... don't depart
God is the same today, yesterday...and always
His Word's still right, His promises true... for you
But if you give up, you'll never know... how to go
Open your eyes wide, receive His blessings, too...
you're due
The answer has come, receive it loudly...
and go proudly!

RHYTHM OF THE SEA

Roaring rhythm of the sea
What is it you'd have us see?
How God said, wait, no further go
Just stop right here, so all will know
That He's the one who charts our ways
And it is not for us to say
We want this, and we want that
And do our enemies "Tit for Tat"
He has timed and laid our path
And has spared us from His Wrath
All we have to do is trust
Keep His ways for they are just
Roaring rhythm of the sea
You confirm God's majesty
With your span so great, so wide
With your ebbs, your flow, your tide
Only God could create you
And have you house the fishes too
You exemplify to man
God's great ways and all He can
When we look on you we know
He's the way that we should go
Here's a thought for all of us
Remember that we're only dust

SKITS

THE REAL MEANING OF EASTER
(A Cantata for Small Children)
By Betty C. Isaac McDaniel

Songs Needed: (Or Equivalents)

1. Jesus Loves the Little Children
2. Go Tell it on the Mountain
3. Because He Lived
4. He Never Said a Word
5. They Crucified My Savior
6. He Arose
7. Glad to Be in His Service

Characters Needed:

Narrator
Young Children
Older Child #1
Older Child #2
Teacher
Choir
False Witness #1
False Witness #2
False Witness #3
Mary
Angel
Preacher

THE PLAY

Narrator: Easter is a special time of the year. Many people have the wrong idea as to what Easter is, and what it's all about. Let's listen in on some children at play; and see if we can find some answers.

Young Children: (They run in playing tag, chasing each other, and making a lot of noise.)

You're it; I caught you; Now I tag you... etc., etc., etc.

Older Child #1: Come on kids. Stop the racket. It's almost time for Sunday School.

Older Child #2: Hey, what are you guys getting for Easter? I'm getting a new dress.

(The children continue to buzz about what they're getting, when the teacher enters.)

Teacher: Alright children. It's time for class. Let's all take our seats.

(Choir begins singing: "Jesus loves the little children", as they take their seats.)

Teacher: (Holds up book and shows some pictures as choir sings.)

Now let us review. Is Easter about getting new clothes?

Children: (Together, loudly) ...NO!

Teacher: Is Easter about the Easter Bunny?

Children…NO!

Teacher: Is Easter about dying eggs?

Children:…NO!

Teacher: Then, what is Easter about?

Choir: (Responds with song: "Go Tell it on the Mountain")

Teacher: Yes, Jesus was born, but why and for what purpose?

Child #1: Starting with Adam, man first sinned and continued to sin.

Child #2: So, God sent his Prophets and Teachers to teach and rescue man, but man wouldn't listen.

Child #1: God had to send his only son, Jesus, to save us from our sins.

Choir: Sings, "Because He Lives".

Child #2: Jesus began to teach the people, heal the sick, and forgive them of all their sins.

Child #1: The religious leaders of that time became jealous and began to accuse him falsely.

They brought him before the High Priest and Leaders, but Jesus never said a word.

Choir: Sings, "He Never Said a Word."

False Witness #1: This man said he was able to destroy the Temple of God, and rebuild it in three days.

False Witness #2: He claimed to be The Christ, and the Son of God.

False Witness #3: That's blasphemy! I say, crucify him, NOW!

False Witnesses #1 and #2: (They grab Jesus and roughly take him out.)

False Witness #3: (Continues to rant and rave and follows them out.)

Choir: Sings, "They Crucified My Savior". (When they get to the 2nd verse, "Sister Mary

she came running", Mary enters...)

Mary: (Runs around looking, and asks...) Where is my Savior? What have you done with him? Where have you taken him?

Angel: He is not here, Mary. He is risen, just like he said.

(Angel comforts Mary and leads her out.)

Choir: Sings, "He Arose!" (With much joy and enthusiasm!)

Preacher: (As choir sings or hums softly) Because Jesus died for our sins, and rose again on the third day, just as he said, we are now again in a right relationship with the Father. Have you accepted forgiveness for your sins and come to Jesus? Don't let this time pass you by... etc.

If you're already saved, you need to find a local church and begin to serve him.

Choir: Concluding song, "Glad to be in His Service".

Narrator: Thanks everyone for coming. Greet your neighbor. Celebrate Easter for the right reasons, and always remember that Jesus died for you!

THE STORY OF JESUS
(A Christmas Play for Children)
Written by: Betty C. Isaac McDaniel

Introduction and General Information:

1. **Play has 21 speaking parts**
   a. Can have as few as 7 speakers
   b. Can have any number between 7 and 21

2. **There are 7 Scenes:**
   a. His birth
   b. His ministry
   c. His betrayal
   d. His crucifixion
   e. His resurrection
   f. His charge to us
   g. The sum of it

3. **Suggestions for presentation:**
   a. Have soft music as children speak
   b. Have a song or Christmas carol between each scene
   c. Children can hold up a picture about their scene
   d. Scenes can be projected on a screen as they speak
   e. Children can act out or mime the events of their scene
   f. Children can wear costumes or dress from their scene

SCENE I–The Birth

Speaker #1

Who is this baby, lying in a manger?
There are no ifs, ands, buts, or maybe
The Virgin gave birth to our Lord

Speaker #2

How did it happen, was it foretold?
Did men and women long behold
That this would come to be?

Speaker #3

John the Baptist went ahead
He told the people they'd be led
By Jesus, the Lion of Judah

Speaker #4

It came to pass as it was stated
God declared, and it was slated
To occur just as He had said

SCENE II–His Ministry

Speaker #5

Jesus picked 12 wise strong men
And told them all to follow Him
To serve and save the people

Speaker #6

Jesus healed and raised the dead

Fed the people and then He led

Them to his Father's grace

Speaker #7

Teaching and preaching and declaring truth

No one needed further proof

That he was the son of God

SCENE III–His Betrayal

Speaker #8

The evil leaders of that day

Did not like what he had to say

And so, they waited to trap him

Speaker #9

Judas, a disciple, and one of the 12

Told the leaders that he would delve

Into ways to help them catch him

Speaker #10

He bargained for 30 pieces of silver

And told them he would go and deliver

His master and teacher to them

Speaker 11

He did what he had bargained for
Then ran to seek an open door
To lead them to our Savior

SCENE IV–His Crucifixion

Speaker 12

They arrested him and said he'd be heard
But Jesus said not a mumbling word
And so, they condemned him to die

Speaker 13

Crucify him! Crucify him! Was what they yelled
His glory and honor were not beheld
So, they took him away to Calvary

Speaker 14

Nailed on a cross between two thieves
Jesus should not have been with any of these
But he submitted to God's perfect will

Speaker 15

Joseph, a disciple, took his body down
And laid it gently on the ground
Then took him away to be buried

SCENE V–His Resurrection

Speaker 16

The women came unto the cave
Where they had said was Jesus' grave
But they were not able to find him

Speaker 17

The grave was there, and stone rolled away
But Jesus was not there that day
And so, they began to cry

Speaker 18

An angel asked them why they sought
The living among the dead?
Dry your eyes, seek your Savior, He's only just ahead

SCENE VI–His Charge to His People

Speaker 19

Finding their Savior alive and well
Oh, what a story they had to tell
To his disciples and all the people

Speaker 20

Jesus said I go to prepare
A place for you and all who care
Proclaim God's love to every man

Speaker 21

Go preach and teach that man should repent
And believe in their hearts that Jesus was sent
To save their very souls.

SCENE VII–The Sum of It

ALL: Do good unto all men
Keep His word and then
We'll live throughout eternity
Together with Him! A-men

(Curtain Call; Take a Bow; Introduce Players; Call to Salvation;
Refreshments/Fellowship).

PLAYS

"ANGEL EYES"
A Christian Play for Children
Written by
Betty Carolyn Isaac McDaniel

INTRODUCTION: This is a Christian Play for children, designed to be produced with simplicity and not a lot of props, costumes or expenses. It is a story about several young "angels" assigned to go down to earth and help various families develop "The Fruit of the Spirit,"

Galatians 5:22-25...says,
"But the fruit of the Spirit is...

LOVE, JOY, PEACE, LONGSUFFERING, GENTLENESS, GOODNESS, FAITH, MEEKNESS, TEMPERANCE...

and they that are Christ's, have crucified the flesh ... and walk in the Spirit"

The proper and prim Head Angel, Sis. Angelic, keeps the angels on task and makes them be accountable. As we know, children will be children, even angelic ones.

It is a Three Act Play:

Act 1–The young Angel Children receive instructions and assignments

Act 2–The children go down to earth to carry out their assignments

Act 3–The children return to heaven to give an account of how they did

ANGEL EYES ACT I
SCENE I

(The play opens with the 8 angels playing "Tag", laughing, talking, patting hands together in a rhyme, etc.)

Sis. Angelic: Children! Children! Time to stop playing. It's time to make our "Cloud Formation", take the role and get our instructions and assignments for the day. Hurry along. Get into formation.

(The children scurry along and rummage through the pile of clouds to get their particular number. [Clouds are numbered 1 through 8] Each cloud is then held at a different level to create a picturesque sky. [Instructions are on the back of the clouds telling them where to hold their clouds, such as — Hold at eye level; waist level, knee level; over their heads, etc.] Sis. Angelic fusses over them and raises and lowers clouds to her liking.)

Sis. Angelic: Very good, children, very good. (Steps back and looks, then frantically...) Where are my rainbows. Rainbows, where are you?

(Two young children run up the aisle, each carrying a half of an arc of the rainbow.)

Children: Here we are! Here we are!

Sis. Angelic: (Fussing over them and placing them in the right order in the middle of the clouds and stepping away to admire her handiwork.)

Oh, you little dears, you form a perfect sky! Just lovely! Just lovely! (Clasping her hands together.)

Sis. Angelic: Alright, it's time to do our opening exercises. (Children moan and roll eyes upward.) Troops, are you ready?

Children: (Dryly) We' re ready...

Sis. Angelic: I can't hear you! Are you READY?

Children: (Loudly and together) ...READY, SISTER ANGELIC!!!

Sis. Angelic: That's better. COUNT OFF...!! Children: (In order) 1 -2 -3 -4 -5 -6 -7 -8!

Sis. Angelic: (Smiling demurely) And of course, (tee hee), I'm "Cloud Nine". O.K., O.K.

(Claps hands) Time for our lesson for the day. Put away your clouds and take your seats so we can get started. Move quickly. We have a long day.

(Small children exit. Others return clouds to their stack and then take a seat on the altar facing Sis. Angelic who now sits in an opposing chair.)

Sis. Angelic: Today we are going to talk about "food" — food for your body and food for your soul.

Angel#1: You mean like "Soul Food"? —- Eggs and grits, and fried chicken and cornbread, and chitlin's and...

Sis. Angelic: (Interrupting) No, no, Angel #1. This is different. We are going to talk about "fruit". First, we'll talk about fruit for your body; (gathers up pictures of fruit), and then we're going to talk about "'The fruit of the Spirit."

Angel #2: What's fruit of the spirit? Is that like a ghost or boogieman?

Sis. Angelic: No, no, no. Nothing like that. Just be patient and we will clear everything up. Now let's give each of you a piece of fruit:

Angel #1- An apple
#2–An orange
#3 -A banana
#4-A peach
#5-A pineapple
#6-A pear
#7- A plum
#8- A bunch of grapes

Sis. Angelic: (Names each fruit as she distributes them to the angels.) Now, what do we do with fruit?

Angel #3: (Waving hand frantically) We hide it away and eat it later, so we don't have to share!

Sis. Angelic: You're kidding, of course. (Angel hangs head)

Angel #4: (Waving hand: frantically) We smush it all together and make a pie!

Sis. Angelic: Maybe the question isn't clear. Here, fill in the blanks:

Fruit is meant to be...EATEN! (Children answer)

So, we can grow big and...STRONG! (Children answer)

Sis. Angelic: Now you have it. Real fruit can be eaten, and it will make you big and strong. Now let's turn our attention to "The Fruit of the Spirit." What do you think that means? And the Spirit is not a boogieman!

(Children ponder and talk amongst themselves. Finally, Angel #5 raises his hand and says)

Angel #5: If the Spirit is not a boogieman, is it a ghost?

Sis. Angelic: You're getting close. The Spirit is sometimes called Ghost, but it's always used as the "Holy Ghost". Let's say that together, childrenHOLY GHOST!

Sis. Angelic: Good. Let's go back to "The Spirit...The Fruit of the Spirit. If real fruit is used to make your body strong, what do you think Spiritual Food does?

Angel #6: (Waving hand frantically) It makes your brain strong!

Sis. Angelic: (A-hem) Not quite, but you're on the right track. It does change us on the inside but not the brain, it changes our(holds up picture of a heart)

Children: (All together) HEART!

Sis. Angelic: (Gushing) You are such brilliant little angels. I love you all. (Throws kisses; children groan and roll eyes up.)

Sis. Angelic: Now, let's go on. Now if the "Fruit of the Spirit" changes your heart, that means you were doing something one way, but when God touches your heart (rubs chest at heart), you begin doing things differently. Example:

If you were mean, you are now...(Children)...NICE

If you were sad, you are now...(Children)...HAPPY

If you had hate for someone, you now have...(Children)...LOVE

Sis. Angelic: Correct. There are nine "Fruit of the Spirit" These are behavior changes that occur when you turn your life over to the Lord; and live to please Him. Look on the back of your fruit card, and there you will see a particular "Fruit of the Spirit". Don't let anyone see your card, because we're going to play a little game and see if they can guess what Spiritual Fruit you have.

(Children turn cards over and take a peek, hiding it from the others.)

Sis. Angelic: In this game, each of you will come up and give a hint, and then see if the others can guess what Spiritual Fruit you are. Here, I'll go first. I used to hate everybody, but now I practice "The Spiritual Fruit" of...(Children together) ...LOVE!

Sis. Angelic: Good! Now let's see one of you try it.

(Angel #6 is madly waving his hand.) Alright #6. Come on up.

Angel #6: Here' s my hint, (he says proudly) I believe I can move mountains... Who am I?

(Angel #8 calls out)

Angel #8: Superman!!

Angel #6: Was Superman given as one of the fruit? You have to pay attention.

(Angel #8 hangs his head)

Angel #6: Alright, here's another clue...Because I believe, I have...

Angel #2: FAITH!

Angel #6: You're right! It's your turn now. Give us a hint about your fruit.

Angel #2: I have perfect...

Angel #5: ATTENDANCE!

Angel #2: Focus. Focus. Attendance was not one of the Fruit of the Spirit. Try again.

I am not at war, I am at...

Angel #5: PEACE!

Angel #2: Good job. Now you come up and share your fruit.

Angel #5: The opposite of badness is?

Angel#4: GOODNESS!

Angel #5: Bingo! You hit the jackpot. Come on up.

Angel #4: I have a very light touch, therefore my fruit is...

Angel #8: Soft and mushy ...A BANANA!

Angel #4: (Frowning) Yeah, right!

Angel #8: Just kidding. It's Gentleness. (Angel #4 nods.) It's my turn!

Angel #8: In order to have this Fruit of the Spirit, you must have self-control...

Angel #1: I know it, but I can' t pronounce it.

Angel #8: What does it sound like?

Angel #1: It sounds like you have a bad temper.

Angel# 8: That's close. But instead of having a bad temper, you have a...

Angel #1: Good temper!

Angel #8: Yes, and that's called TEMPERANCE. You have self-control. You don't fly off the handle easily. It's your turn.

Angel #1: If I am very, very, happy, I am...

Angel #8: On drugs?

Angel #1: Stop clowning around. Let's see, how about this. I love everybody and things are going my way, I am filled with...

Angel #7: JOY!

Angel #1: That's right! Come on up.

Angel #7: I'm not loud, and sometimes I look at the floor. Who am I?

Angel #8: Somebody looking for money on the floor?

Angel #7: You're so corny! Anybody else?

Angel #3: MEEKNESS!

Angel #7: Now that's the right answer. It's your turn.

Angel #3: When times are hard, I don' t complain. I take things in stride.

(Angel #8: Frantically waves his hand)

Children: Forget it 8. Don't even try it!

Angel #4: (Proudly) You don't mind suffering; it's called LONGSUFFERING

Angel #3: That's right. Good for you.

Sis. Angelic: Good for ALL of you. You did a fine job, except for a few off the wall, I mean off the sky (tee hee), answers, you all did just fine.

Sis. Angelic: Since you worked so hard, why don't we take a little break and come back a little later and get our assignments for the day.

Children: Yippee! Yippee! (All of them run down the aisles and out.)

Sis. Angelic: (Gathering up all of her items). Angel work is such hard work, but it's... "Heavenly" (tee hee). Lovely, lovely, lovely...

(Exits with a flare)

End of Act 1

Act II
SCENE I

The scene opens with the children again playing and chattering. Sis. Angelic calls to them.

Sis. Angelic: Children! Children! Break time is over. Come along now. (Children grudgingly break up their play and move towards Sis. Angelic.)

Sis. Angelic: Hurry, hurry, children. We have a busy day today...Do we need the cloud formation?

Children: (Emphatically) NO!

Sis. Angelic: Do we need the countdown?

Children: NO!

Sis. Angelic: (Dejectedly) Alright, alright. Let's move on to your assignments.

Let's see..., hmm... I think I'll put you into groups of two each, and let each group go to a different family. Your job will be to sprinkle them with 'angel dust' so that they can see through your lovely "Angel Eyes," the Fruit of the Spirit that you have, and that they need. Let's see... Angels 4 and 7, you're Gentleness and Meekness; come forward and get your assignment. (Children step up.) Let me put your fruit on you (pins them on or places a collar on them over their heads with their particular 'Fruit of the Spirit' written on both sides, front and back.)

Sis. Angelic: Now you two are going down to Pottstown, Pennsylvania, to look up the ("Loud-and-Pushy-<u>Palmers</u>") and get them on the road to being gentle and meek. Take your bag of 'angel dust' (tee, hee), and sprinkle it over their heads, and they will begin to see as your angel eyes see, your particular Fruit of the Spirit. (Hands them the address written down, and two bags of 'angel dust'. The two examine items and discuss them amongst themselves and begin to exit to their assignment.)

Sis. Angelic: (Calling after them) And remember, if all else fails—Call on the Holy Ghost to help you. (Points to the back where a tall young man in a white robe flashes a big smile and flexes his muscles. The two angels giggle and exit, while the other angels give the Holy Ghost a big cheer!

Sis. Angelic: O.K. now... <u>Longsuffering and Temperance</u>, come on up. (<u>Angels 3 & 6,</u> come forward) You're going to Yardley, Pennsylvania and sprinkle the ("I've-Got-to Have-it-Yesterday-<u>Youngs</u>"). This family can surely use your fruit. (Pins signs on both) Here's the address (Hands them paper. They chatter and point to address, etc., and exit).

Sis. Angelic: <u>Numbers 1 and 5, Joy and Goodness</u>, here's your assignment. (Pins on fruit) You're going to Dover, Delaware to the ("Down-in-the-Dumps-<u>Dawsons</u>"). Take your angel dust, and don't spare any. (Angels examine slip and exit)

Sis. Angelic: Now for my <u>last two dears, 2 & 8</u>. We've saved the best for you. There's a family in Tyler, Texas that needs your fruit: <u>Love and Peace</u>, so that they will have more <u>Faith</u>...

They are the ("Troubled-and-Touchy-<u>Thompsons</u>"). Go down and sprinkle them generously and give them a bunch. Remember, if all else fails, call on the "Holy Ghost!" (They smile, chatter and exit).

Sis. Angelic: By George, I believe they've got it. (Gathering her things) Angel work, angel work — there's nothing like it. I think I'll go help myself to some "Angel Food Cake" (tee, hee). I've earned a treat today. (Exits)

*NOTE: The following Scenes; 2, 3, 4 and 5, may be omitted, depending upon your pool of actors, and their ages, and any time restraint you may have; or small children who are unable to remember their lines. If this is the case, go immediately to the last act, ACT III.

Act II
SCENE II

(Angels "Gentleness" and "Meekness" enter down the middle aisle and go to the left where they find the ("Loud and Pushy <u>Palmers</u>") going at it.)

Wife: "It ain't gonna happen! Not in this life, nor the life to come! What makes you think you can always have your way? It's my time now!"

Husband: When did I ever have my way? It's always—Your way, or the highway—

Wife: Don't even try it. Who insisted that we buy a new car when we didn't even need it!

Husband: We did need it. That old car was shot!

(As the Palmers continue to argue, the angels sprinkle angel dust first on the wife, who immediately changes her tone (mid-sentence) to a softer, and kinder one. The husband is amazed and comments, sarcastically...)

Husband: What happened? Did you run out of steam? I guess your bitter tongue got tired of spewing out acid, and...(The angels sprinkle him with dust and he too immediately changes his tone. They exit hugging, talking nicely to each other, and vowing not to be mean to each other again, apologizing, etc. The angels give each other the high five salute, the victory sign, and exit smiling and complementing each other.)

SCENE Ill

(Angels "Longsuffering" and "Temperance" enter down the center aisle and go to the right, where they come upon the ("I' ve-got-to-have-it-yesterday, -<u>Youngs</u>"), whining and complaining about their lot.)

Daughter: How come I can't have a pair of Princess boots that all the girls are wearing?

Mother: Because you already have boots that are practically new, and besides, I need a new stove. This old one has had it. I should have bought one a long time ago!

Son: (Whining) Everybody always gets things before me. I've been asking for a new jacket, and nobody pays me any mind!

The whining goes on and on. One of the angels sprinkles the daughter with dust, whose tone changes immediately. The other two look at her in amazement, until they too are sprinkled. They all then exit, smiling and vowing to compromise with each other and be patient about the things they want, letting the other get what they want first, etc.)

First Angel: Boy! I didn't know how that was going to go.

Second Angel: Me neither. (Then, jokingly) Here...let me sprinkle some angel dust on you so that you'll always be nice to me.

First Angel: (Playfully) Not a chance! (Begins to run out giggling with Second Angel in hot pursuit, laughing and throwing angel dust after him as they exit.)

SCENE IV

(Angels "Joy" and "Goodness" enter by the left side aisle and come upon the ("Down-in the-dumps-Dawsons"), sitting around the kitchen table lamenting.)

Husband: Boy, am I in a downer. Why does everything happen to me? I just knew I was going to get that promotion, but they gave it to someone under me!

Wife: You think you have troubles...at least you have a job! I can't even find one! And we have all these bills to pay!

Daughter: I guess that lets me out for new sneakers. I should have known I wouldn't get them.

(Angels sprinkle Mother and daughter, whose tones change immediately, but the Husband jumps up and begins pacing back and forth and the angels can't reach him.)

Husband: Easy for you two to change your tones, but what about me? I tell you I should have gotten that promotion, etc., etc., etc.)

(Angels realize their situation is helpless. The father is just too tall! Then they remember what Sis. Angelic said, and they both say in unison...)

Angels: Holy Ghost! Holy Ghost! Help! Help!

(The Holy Ghost runs down the aisle and picks up Angel One, who quickly sprinkles, then pours the rest of the bag on Father, whose tone immediately changes. The Holy Ghost flexes and bows to the angels and runs out. The angels giggle and cheer.

Meanwhile the family, lovingly and upbeat, exits.)

Angel One: That was a close one!

Angel Two. Thank God for the Holy Ghost. Let's run and find Him and thank Him for His help.

(The two run out calling for the Holy Ghost.)

SCENE V

(The last two angels, "Love, Peace, and Faith" enter by the right aisle, talking and looking at the address and commenting that they have to find the "Troubled-and-Touchy-Thompsons". They arrive at the house up front.)

First Angel: Here it is. (Peers in the window, with other angel)

Second Angel: It looks like no one is home.

First Angel: Let's look around the side of the house.

Second Angel: (After they look) Not only are they not at home, it looks like they have moved out. I don't see any furniture.

First Angel: Me neither. What are we going to do? How will we find them? We can't complete our mission unless we find them.

Neighbor: A-hem! Looking for the Thompsons? (Angels nod) Well, you're too late. They moved out last week. Strange bunch they were, very sensitive and very troubled. Why I remember one time when...

Angel One: (Cutting him off) Can you tell us where to find them?

Angel Two: It's very important that we find them.

Neighbor: Well, you go down this road for about 2 miles, past the old oak tree. Then you veer left by Snookums Bar and Grill, then you make a left down Memory Lane past the old cemetery, hook a sharp right and go about 4 miles further, and they should be the first shack, I mean the first house, on the left.

Angel One: We'll never find them.

Angel Two: It's a lost cause.

Neighbor: I'll say. Well good luck to you anyway. Got to run. See you around. (Exits)

Angels together: Help! Holy Ghost, help! Help!

(Holy Ghost enters with a flair. Leans down to hear the angels' dilemma. They point, hunch their shoulders, etc. The Holy Ghost motions them to follow Him. He leads them around the church, bent over for secrecy, children bend and follow, looking over their shoulders, etc. After weaving up and down the aisles, the Holy Ghost points to a house.)

Angel One: Oh, thank you Holy Ghost. We would never have found our way if it weren't for you. (Holy Ghost smiles and flexes.)

Second Angel: God bless you. Oh, I forgot, you are God. Well give yourself a blessing.

You're worthy!

(Holy Ghost smiles and exits.) Angels wave good-by. They open the door where they find the Thompsons sitting around and blaming each other for their troubles.

Mama: We lost the house because of you!

Papa: It wasn't me. It was because of your no-good brother who moved in and bummed off of us for nine months; eating and drinking and paying no rent!

Mama: Don't talk about my brother. How about the time your sister came to stay and didn't know when to leave!

Papa: At least she didn't eat as much as your brother.

Mama: (Begins to sob in her handkerchief) You always blame me for everything.

(Papa starts out gruff, but the angels quickly sprinkle him, at which time his tone changes considerably. Mama jumps up before the angels can sprinkle her, and she continues pacing and sobbing into her handkerchief. The angels can't reach her now or keep up with her.)

Angels: (Together) Help, Holy Ghost. We need you again!

(Enter the tall and handsome Holy Ghost again. Flexing and smiling he leans down to hear from the angels, who point frantically at Mama, who is sobbing and going up and down the aisles. As she nears the Holy Ghost, He puts His foot out and Mama stumbles and falls. The angels quickly sprinkle her before she gets up. The Holy Ghost gives the thumbs up sign and exits smiling and flexing. The angels smile and wave, as Mama gets up with a brand new, attitude. Father quickly comes over to assist, and they both exit in a kind and loving way. The angels are standing by with folded hands and big smiles.

Angel One: Boy, was that close!

Angel Two: You're telling me! Did you see the Holy Ghost trip her? That was something.

Angel One: But you know, sometimes you have to fall down to appreciate getting up.

Angel Two: That's right. You're absolutely right.

Angel One: Now how do we get out of here? (Pointing) Was it around the oak tree or the cemetery at Memory Lane?

Angel Two: I thought it was 2 miles past Snookums Bar and Grill! (Points over there)

Angels: (Together) Help! Holy Ghost! Help! (They run off stage exiting, holding their heads ("Home Alone" style), and still calling on the Holy Ghost).

End of Act II

ANGEL EYES
Act III

Sis. Angelic: (Waving and motioning) Angels! Dear, Angels! It's time to come and give an account of yourselves. Bring your reports. Come quickly! Line up for your cloud formation.

(Angels scurry along and dig into box for their particular cloud. Sis. Angelic shoos them along. They find their clouds and line up.)

Sis. Angelic: (Fussing and arranging clouds to her liking.) Where are my rainbows?

Rainbows? Come along, hurry, hurry!

Sis. Angelic: (Placing the rainbows, then standing back and admiring her handiwork.) Lovely, lovely. Just...heavenly. (tee hee)

Sis. Angelic: Alright. Let's put our clouds away. Thank you rainbows. (They smile and exit.) Let's all take our seats so you can give your reports. (All sit)

Sis. Angelic: Who wants to go first and tell us about their adventures? (All frantically call out and wave their hands... me! me! me!, etc.)

Sis. Angelic: My, my! Tell you what we'll do...we'll go in order. Let's see...Gentleness and Meekness, please stand. (They oblige, smiling at the others because they' re first.) How did your assignment go with the "Pushy Palmers" in Pottstown, PA?

Meekness: Once we hit them with that angel dust, they became very gentle and polite.

Gentleness: Yes. It was a complete transformation. Mission accomplished. No problems!

Sis. Angelic: Very good. Just the kind of report I like to hear. You may be seated.

Sis. Angelic: Now, let' s hear from "<u>Temperance and Longsuffering</u>. (They quickly stand) What did the "I've-got-to-have-it-yesterday, Young's" do?

Temperance: After their dusting, they became new creatures.

Longsuffering: Yeah, before we knew it, the Young's were compromising, and working together in love, each vowing to let the other's desires go before theirs.

Sis. Angelic: A success story if I ever heard one. Great job, and you may be seated.

Sis. Angelic: Now let's hear from <u>Joy and Goodness</u>. (They stand) Was your trip as wonderful as the others?

Joy: Well, not exactly.

Goodness: The "Down-in-the-dumps, <u>Dawsons</u>" were putting each other down, blaming each other, and were without a ray of hope.

Joy: Yeah, we knew they needed a sprinkling, fast! We immediately went to work and had just about everybody sprinkled and changing their tune...when the father jumped up and we couldn't reach him!

Sis. Angelic: Oh, my!

Other Angels: What happened? What did you do?

Joy: Hold your horses...I mean your wings (tee hee). We're getting to it. We did what Sis. Angelic told us to do...

Joy and Goodness: (Together) We called on the Holy Ghost! (Children grin and cheer and clap their hands. Sis. Angelic gushes.)

Goodness: Then quicker than you could say, "Jack Johnson", he picked Joy up and she dumped the rest of the bag on father. And as they say, the rest was history!

Sis. Angelic: What a great story. Good job. I'm very proud of you. (They smile and are seated).

Sis. Angelic: O.K. "Faith" and "Peace". Did your family find Love? Can you top that story?

Peace: Can we!

Faith: How much time do we have?

Sis. Angelic: (Looking horrified) Oh, my! Is it that bad?

Faith: Not so much bad as, let's just say, interesting

Peace: To say the least.

Sis. Angelic: Well, let's just get on with it. Don't keep us in suspense. Who wants to start?

Faith: I'll start. First, once we found the house of the "Troubled Thompsons", we looked inside, and nobody was home.

Peace: Not only were they not at home, the house was completely empty... no furniture, no people...nothing!

Angels: Oh, no! Wow! Gosh!

Sis. Angelic: Then what did you do?

Faith: We didn't know what to do! Then a neighbor came over and told us that they had recently moved!

Peace: We were horrified. Then the neighbor tried to give us directions to their new house, or as he put it, their new shack!

Angels: That wasn't good. That wasn't nice, etc. etc.

Faith: If you think that was bad, you should have heard the directions he gave us on how to find them! It sounded like gibberish and doubletalk.

Peace: Yeah, go down to the old oak tree and turn down Cemetery Lane!

Faith: Not Cemetery Lane...Memory Lane!

Peace: Sorry. Anyway... then he said we had to find "Snookums Bar and Grill", as our next landmark!

Sis. Angelic: Oh, dear. It sounds like you were in a terrible place. Did you ever find them?

Faith: Not on our own; we couldn't do it. We had to...

Faith and Peace: (Together)Call on the Holy Ghost!

(Angels clap and cheer)

Sis. Angelic: Did everything go well after that?

Peace: Well... almost. After we found the poor 'Troubled Thompsons', there they sat, poor and troubled, and they were going at it. The mother was blaming the father for letting them lose the house, and he was blaming her deadbeat brother for staying with them and not paying rent!

Faith: Yeah, and they were going on and on until we managed to sprinkle the husband and he changed his tune, but the mother had gotten up sobbing and was wandering all over the place.

Angels: What did you do? What happened? etc., etc.

Peace: We did what any other good angel would do in a tight spot, we...

Faith and Peace: (Together) Called on the Holy Ghost!

(Angels cheer and clap)

Sis. Angelic: I bet that did the trick for you.

Faith: Well, again, almost. We know that God's ways aren't always our ways, but it knocked us for a loop when the Holy Ghost *tripped* the wife!

Sis. Angelic: (In horror) You mean the Holy Ghost knocked her down? Was she hurt?

Peace: No...but it was a good fall and for a good reason. You see, once she went down, we were able to sprinkle her with the angel dust.

Sis. Angelic: Oh, my! Thank goodness!

Faith: And the way we saw it was, sometimes you have to fall down, so you can look up. So if you fall down, look up; then you can sit up.

Peace: And if you can sit up, then you can get up.

Faith: And if you can get up, then you can look up.

Peace: And when you look up, look to Jesus.

Peace and Faith: (Together) ...The Author and Finisher of our Faith!

(Both smile and slap each other a high five.)

Sis. Angelic: (Sadly) I'm speechless. You angels are wise beyond your years. I guess you don't need me anymore. (Looks downcast)

Angels: (Rushing to Sis. Angelic and mobbing her with hugs and kisses) No, no, Sis. Angelic. We love you. We need you. You taught us everything that we know!

(Sis. Angelic gushes and smiles.)

Goodness: (Breaking away) I know; let's do our theme song that Sis. Angelic taught us.

That will cheer her up!

Angels: Yeah, yeah!. (Rush back to their places and get into formation. Sis. Angelic smiling, sits down.)

Goodness: Alright. Troops are you ready?

Angels: READY!

(Angels do their "Theme Song", starting with the Chant, which is done to a Cadence, "Army Style"; half of the children (1-4) starting the chant, and numbers (5-8) repeating what they say, and so on until it's finished; then leading into the song which is done with much animation, swaying and movement. Synchronized steps on the refrain are good, or any other creative touch to have a bang up ending! At the very last finale line of the song, the two center angels, numbers 4 and 5, reach down and bring Sis. Angelic up to stand in the middle and take part in the last line of the song and play. She too sings, You' ll...Have...Angel...Eyes!!! All hold hands and raise them together, letting go when all hands are above their heads, at which time they all wave or shake their hands on the closing note. They may join hands again and take a bow.)

Theme Song

I. Chant

(Divide group in half: four and four)

1. We are angels from above (Point up)...Other half of children repeat the line, etc.
2. We can help you practice love (Cross hands on heart)

3. Love is what you want to do (Hand on heart then point out to audience)

4. When it seems life' s tough to you (Cover ears and frown)

5. Keep your eyes on what is right (Shade eyes and look around)

6. God will give you strength and might (Flex arm muscles)

7. Don't forget to watch and pray (Hands in prayer/ Look around)

8. Read the Word throughout the day (Hands in prayer, then open them)

9. Then when trouble hunts you down (Scrunch/Look over shoulder)

10. You won't have to cry and frown (Frown and wipe tears)

11. You will know just what to do (Smile and nod yes)

12. Practice peace and patience too (Tilt head and rest on hands)

13. Then you'll help your fellow man (Hands down then lift them up)

14. You will help him take a stand (Half turn, stand tall)

15. Then he'll look to God above (Hands up and look up)

16. God who is the Gift of Love (EVERYONE RECITE 16 TOGETHER)

-And slowly cross arms on chest then open them towards audience-

II. SONG

(Go immediately into the song, "Angel Eyes"
   after a short lead-in by the pianist)

(dah, dah...dah, dah, dah, dah...dah)

(Can be sung to any song or tune; Can be read or rapped;
Can be omitted.)

"ANGEL EYES"

Angel eyes, angel eyes, angel eyes; We've got
Angel eyes, angel eyes, angel eyes
We can see all that we should
And we do all that is good,
Cause we've got
Angel eyes, angel eyes, angel eyes
Cause we've got
Angel eyes, angel eyes, angel eyes
We went down to that old earth
And we spread some joy and mirth
Cause we've got Angel eyes, angel eyes, angel eyes
Cause we've got Angel eyes, angel eyes, angel eyes
When we gave them angel dust
Then they did just what they must
Cause we've got
Angel eyes, angel eyes, angel eyes
Cause we've got

Angel eyes, angel eyes, angel eyes
You can share in their joy too
Let His word fall over you And you'll have
Angel eyes, angel eyes, angel eyes
You'll have angel eyes
Angel eyes, angel eyes, angel eyes...
YOU'LL... HAVE... ANGELEYES!!!
(Wave and/or shake hands above your head)
(Bow and take another bow you earned it!)

The Accountability Seat of Christ
better known as...
"THE HOT SEAT"
Written by
Betty Carolyn Isaac McDaniel

Introduction:

The play is a comedy about eight people who have died and are trying to get into heaven. But first, they must confront St. Peter at the Pearly Gates, a stern but comical man who separates the "Good Seed" from the "Bad", by looking into the "Book of Life" and flashbacks of their lives while they were down on the earth.

This is a completely new work, including the songs and the raps. All materials are copyrighted and cannot be used without the expressed permission of the author. Also, if any educators or teachers would like to use this book as a teaching tool, a Study Guide may be obtained by contacting me as follows:

Mrs. Betty C. Isaac McDaniel
11 Pinewood Lane
Sicklerville, New Jersey 08081
(856) 728-9446

God bless you, and may you touch many lives as you minister to God's people through drama.

"THE HOT SEAT"

MAIN CHARACTERS:

ST. PETER: Keeper of Heaven's Gates. Screens everyone who comes.

SLICK WILLY: Street-smart hoodlum heading straight to hell.

REV. JUDSON: Holier-than-thou corrupt minister.

MOTHER WYNONA: Led a good Christian life while on earth.

MISS THANG: Reformed hooker; converted at the last minute.

MISSIONARY MARVA: Self-serving, dishonest worker.

VOLUNTEER: Works with Missionary Marva.

TOM: Rich man who became poor to save others.

POLICEMAN: Warns Tom about the wicked, evil streets.

OLDER MAN: Man trying to go to Heaven on his Momma's prayers.

YOUNGER MAN: Trying to go to Heaven on his Poppa's prayers.

OTHERS:

NARRATOR: Does opening introduction of play.

VOICE: Does the opening and closing lines.

GUARDS: Men in black who drag the unsaved off the stage.

PRAISE TEAM: Those in white who clap and dance the saved into heaven.

PERSONS: For the Street Scene.

PERSONS: For the Church Scene.

HOOKERS: For the Street Scene.

SIS. BRAXTON: Rev. Judson's "Other Interest".

ALSO NEEDED:

MUSICIANS/SINGERS

MIME or DANCER

RAPPER

DRUMMER

SOUND EFFECTS PERSON
STAGEHANDS

LIGHTS PERSON/ CURTAINS, TECH. PEOPLE

"HOT SEAT SIGN"

"Enter and be seated...
  If you can!"

PROPS

LARGE SEAT

LARGE TELEPHONE BOOK

PODIUM

TABLE OR DESK

TWO SIGNS:

"ST. PETER"

"HOT SEAT"

BIBLE

BLACK ROBES

WHITE ROBES

PLAY MONEY

BAGS OF DRUGS

WHISKEY BOTTLES

SLIPS OF PAPERS WITH NAMES

"THE HOT SEAT"

A Breakdown of the Scenes:

ACT I
Scene I
1. Voice
2. People (Cast Members)
3. Drummer
4. Musicians or Sound Effects

Scene II
1. St. Peter
2. Slick Willy
3. Drug Dealers & Hookers
4. Guards (Men in Black)

Scene III
1. St. Peter
2. Rev. Judson
3. Rapper
4. Church Members
5. Guards (Men in Black)

Scene IV
1. St. Peter
2. Mother Wynona
3. Music ("I Feel Good" by James Brown)
4. Praise Team

Scene V
1. St. Peter
2. Miss Thang
3. Hookers

4. Street People

5. Praise Team

(Intermission)

ACT II

Scene I

1. St. Peter

2. Missionary

3. Volunteer

4. Guards

Scene II

1. Singer

2. Mime or Dancer

Scene III

1. St. Peter

2. Tom

3. Burns (3-4)

4. Policeman

5. Praise Team

Scene IV

1. St. Peter

2. Older Man

3. Younger Man

4. Rapper

5. Praise Team and Cast

6. Grand Finale

Scene V

1. St. Peter

2. Voice

"The Accountability Seat of Christ"

better known as...
"THE HOT SEAT"

Narrator: Gives a general welcome and introduction.

II Corinthians 5:10 tells us that... "We must all appear before the Judgment Seat of Christ, that everyone may receive the things done in his body, according to that he hath done, whether it be good or bad".

The Gospel can be presented in many forms, from preaching and teaching, music and poetry, to drama and rap, and even in humor. Proverbs 15:13 tells us, "A merry heart maketh a cheerful countenance". And Proverbs 17:22 says, "A merry heart doeth good like a medicine".

So, sit back and take a dose of merriment medicine, as we present to you...

"THE HOT SEAT"
A humorous work, but with serious consequences...!
—Curtains, drum roll, music, etc.—

ACT I
SCENE I

VOICE: "And God said to be fruitful and multiply and replenish the earth.

And love thy neighbor as thyself."...

(People begin to drift onto the stage, very friendly, laughing, talking and shaking hands. Babies are wheeled on; younger children play ball, tag, etc.)

—DRUM ROLL— (All freeze)

"But God repented that He had made man, for the heart of man was continually evil!"

(Friendliness now turns to corruption and violence. Some shoot or stab each other. Others fist fight, take drugs, steal, drink out of a paper bag, etc.)

—DRUM ROLL— (All freeze)

"For it is appointed unto men once to die**! (DRUM ROLL)** but after that —**The Judgment!!!—**"

(Shrill cries, gun shots, moans, etc.)

(Stage clears and curtain is drawn)

SCENE II

ST. PETER:

(St. Peter enters, yawns, stretches. He busies around straightening up, mutters and puts the "R" back in his name sign, which reads "St. Pete_". He cleans his glasses, dusts off the "hot seat", mumbles about a busy day and that he has to judge seven souls. Lays out a big telephone book (covered over with the title, "The Book of Life", lays it on a stand, peers into it, then yells—-) ... "Who' s first?"

SLICK WILLY: (Street-smart dude heading straight for hell!)

"Hey... St. Pete. Wud up? Gimme some skin. They said this wouldn't take long, that all you had to do was to sign off on this slip of paper so I can ease on into heaven and get that long white robe and slide right on into eternity for that good life. Here you go, sign right here." (Tries to hand slip to St. Peter...)

ST. PETER: "Hold it. Not so fast young man. And what is this new talk that this generation has? What is 'wud up' and 'gimme some skin'?"

SLICK WILLY: "Well, you see, St. Pete, back in the day..."

ST. PETER: (Interrupting)... "Never mind. Never mind. Now what did you say your name was?"

SLICK WILLY: "My real name is William Widener, but all my friends call me 'Slick Willy'. You can call me Willy. We're friends, aren't we? Gimme some skin St. Pete... (Puts out hand which St. Peter ignores, and begins to look up his name in the big book.)

ST. PETER: "Let me see, Widener, is that with one or two E's?"

SLICK WILLY: "Two E's. (Spells it out.) W-I-D-E-N-E-R, William. (Emphasizes the E's.)

Look hard. I know it's there."

ST. PETER: (Slaps the book closed.) "Sorry. I don't see it..."

SLICK WILLY: (Getting more serious.) "Hold it. Hold it. I know I'm in there. Are you sure you didn't make a mistake? Did you spell it right? Here, let me take a look." (Reaches for the book.)

ST. PETER: (Pulling the book away.) "That won't be necessary. I read very well. Thank you very much. But here... Tell you what I'll do. We'll roll back the "Tape of Time" and take a first-hand look at one of your 'typical days' while down there on earth. Fair enough?"

SLICK WILLY: "Attaboy. You'll see. I was a good person. Just had a few rough breaks here and there. Had to hustle for a living you know, and..."

ST. PETER: (With a loud and interrupting voice...) "ROLL THE TAPE!"

—Drum Roll—

(Lights dim, pan in on a street scene. Slick Willy is seen hustling people, yelling at his prostitutes about getting to work and bringing in his money, passing out drugs and dirty money, etc. Gun shots are heard, flashing lights, confusion...)

—Drum Roll—

(Pans back to St. Peter and Slick Willy)

ST. PETER: "I've seen enough. Guards! (Enter the Men in Black, and they drag Slick Willy off the stage, who is kicking and screaming and protesting his fate. St. Peter looks away and yells...) Next...!!!"

SCENE III

(Enter the next to be judged, obviously a minister with his clergy collar, Bible in hand and a "holier-than-thou" air about him.)

ST. PETER: "And you are...?"

REV. JUDSON: "I am the Right Rev., Dr. Emeritus Willard S. P. Judson the III, B.A., B.B., M.A., V.S.T., Q.R.S., etc., etc. Surely you have heard of me. I was the pastor of the 'Greater Mt. Nebo Universal Church of the Nazarene...'"

ST. PETER: "Sir, we're not interested in your titles, but in your life!" (Looking in the Book of Life.) Now how do you spell your last name?

REV. JUDSON: "Judson... J-U-D-S-O-N. (Hands him his slip.) It should only take you a minute or two to find that. I'm POSITIVE I'm in there. Why we held more revivals every year, sold more chicken dinners on Friday nights... Course we used to swing a little bit on Saturdays, and..."

ST. PETER: "Here we go... Judson. Judson, B., Judson, K., Judson, R., Judson, V., Judson, Z. Sorry. You're not listed." (Closes the book with a snap and raises his hand to signal the guards...)

REV. JUDSON: "You're kidding, aren't you? All those chicken dinners I sold!

All those raffles and Bingo games! Check again. You probably just overlooked it..." (Jumps up out of the chair.)

ST. PETER: (With obvious annoyance.) Is that seat too hot to sit in? Every body keeps jumping up out of it! Tell you what. Why don't we just listen to this "Hot Seat Rap".

(Rapper enters and does this rap:)

THE HOT SEAT RAP

Is that seat too hot to sit
Does it feel like fire's been lit
Lit to scorch your very soul
Cause the Bible although told
Was pushed aside not to abide
And off you went 'cause you were bent
On your wicked ways
Is that seat too hot to take
Does it make you shake and quake
Cause you know you didn't do
All that was required of you
You just pushed The Bible aside
You didn't even try to hide

Your wicked ways
If you'd do what God asked you
Then you wouldn't have to shrink
Scratch your head and try to think
Am I in or am I out
What's my fate or what's my lot
You would know beyond a doubt
Jump and shout you made it in

(Rapper exits saying..."Must be a hot seat...Must be a hot seat...")

REV. JUDSON: "I did all of that. I was a good person!"

ST. PETER: "ROLL THE TAPE!"

—Drum Roll—

(Pans to a church scene. Church has just let out. a few of the ladies and members remain chatting. Rev. Judson is seen slipping some of the collection money into his pocket. He falsifies some receipts, gives them to the Deacon, walks over to the ladies, inappropriately hugging, them, winking at his favorite, and slips her a note.)

REV. JUDSON: "Now you ladies run along. Sis. Brackston and I have to... take care of a little business." (Puts his arm around her and leads her to an exit. Remaining women giggle and head for the other exit. Pans back to St. Peter.)

ST. PETER: "I've seen enough... GUARDS! (Men in Black drag a protesting Rev. Judson off the stage.) ... Next!"

SCENE IV

MOTHER WYNONA: (Meekly) "Good morning, Sir. Nice day, isn't it?" (Hands 'name slip' to St. Peter, who only mutters...)

ST. PETER: "I suppose you're positive that your name's in here too. This should be quick and easy. Your last name's ' Scott', right?" (Continues looking for her name.)

MOTHER WYNONA: "Yes, sir." (Meekly)

ST. PETER: "Scott, B.; Scott, Wilson; Scott... How do you spell your first name?"

MOTHER WYNONA: " W-Y-N-0 -N-A, sir."

ST. PETER: Scott, Winston; Scott, Wynona!!! Well, praise the Lord! Congratulations, my dear. You have just made it into heaven!!!!

(Music blares out James Brown's "I Feel Good".) Praise Team comes out clapping and shouting and trying to crown Mother Wynona, who is now doing flips, moon walking, throwing off her old clothes, does the running man, etc. They finally catch up with her and drape a long white robe on her, as she shouts on out into heaven.)

ST. PETER: (Smiling broadly after Mother Wynona.) "Now that's what I'm talking about! (Still looking after Mother Wynona, he calls and motions for the next person.) Next...! Yes sir, Godly women who lead a good and moral life and have been a blessing to their families and churches throughout the years, and..." (Turns around to see "Miss Thang" with high top boots and a VERY, short skirt, or hot pants, on.)

ST. PETER: "Good Lord, woman! Where's the rest of your clothing?"

MISS THANG: "I'm sorry, sir; but this was what I was wearing when I was...ahem, on my way to work."

ST. PETER: "What kind of WORK did you do?"

MISS THANG: (Embarrassedly) "I... I... was a hooker."

ST. PETER: "Oh, you used to put things on hooks, like an assembly line in a factory?"

MISS THANG: "No... I was more into 'sales'"

ST. PETER: "Oh, you sold things. How nice. What did you sell?"

MISS THANG: (Mumbles) "My body."

ST. PETER: "I can't hear you. Speak up, child. It's alright."

MISS THANG: (A little louder, but clearly.) "My body."

ST. PETER: (Aghast) "YOUR BODY!! You sold your body? You mean you were a... a..." (Pretending to faint and fans himself.)

MISS THANG: (Interrupting)" But I repented! I accepted Jesus Christ as my Savior!"

ST. PETER: (Hand on chin) "Hmm... So, you say. Let's just take a look.

ROLL THE TAPE!"

—Drum Roll—

(Pans to a street scene. Hookers are hustling passers-by. They see Miss Thang and wave to her to join them)

MISS THANG: "I can't go with you. I've quit the business. I'm saved now.

I just got saved at Rev. Hampton's church tonight. I've given it up. I'm going to lead a clean life for Jesus now."

(Girls laugh sarcastically and say, "Good luck!" She waves back to them not looking where she's going and walks into the street and is hit by a car...) Horns honk, lights flash on and off, drum roll, etc. (Pans back to St. Peter)

ST. PETER: Hmmm... "Very interesting. But I've been looking, and I can't seem to find your name under 'Miss Thang'."

MISS THANG: "Oh, I'm sorry. That was my street name. My real name is Shakia Braxton".

ST. PETER: "Oh. I was looking under the ' M' s' . Let's see... B-Br-Bra (Miss Thang has fingers crossed and praying.) Braf-Brak-Bram Brax—ton. Well, who would have thunk it. You really did make it in!"

(Miss Thang is grinning and jumping up and down and clapping her hands.)

ST. PETER: "Well, you know we can't give you a long white robe or crowns.

You are a new Saint who ' barely', and I mean ' barely' (looking at short outfit) made it in, but you did make it in."

(Motions for Praise Team who come out with less fanfare than before. They give a weak clap and mild shouts of joy and put on her a TRULY SHORT ROBE. Miss Thang doesn't' t care; she's proud she at least made it in and continues to shout and dance her way off stage. Praise Team follows dryly.)

ST. PETER: (Calling after her while picking up his book and other items.) "You'll probably have to tug at it all through eternity, but you DID make it in!" (Exits)

—Drum Roll, Music, Curtains—

–—I N T E R M I SSION—-

ACT II
SCENE: 1

(Scene opens with St. Peter again putting his "R" back up, mumbling, dusting, straightening up, etc.)

ST. PETER: "NEXT!" (Continues to straighten up, opens the big book, etc., as the haughty missionary comes in.) "And who might you be?"

MISSIONARY: "Why, I'm Marva McIlvany, the missionary to Kenya? Don't you know me?"

ST. PETER: "Can't say that I do."

MISSIONARY: "Why I spent years and years on the mission field, serving unselfishly and giving to others, and..."

ST. PETER: (Who has been looking in the book as she spoke.) "I've been looking for your name here and I can't seem to find it."

(Missionary looks horrified! St. Peter pats her on the shoulder.) "Tell you what... why don't we just turn back the hands of time and take a look at your (coughs) "pristine" life. Have a seat here; it's not too hot is it?"

MISSIONARY: "Oh, no. The seat's not too hot?" **ST. PETER:** "ROLL THE TAPE!"

—Drums, lights flash on and off, etc.—

(Pans to a scene in Africa. Marva is recording donations and pocketing most. One of the volunteers runs in.)

VOLUNTEER: "Missionary Marva! Come quick! One of the townspeople has been bitten by a snake!"

MISSIONARY MARVA: "Not now! Not now! Tell them, I'm busy. I'm counting my money... I mean the mission's money. I have to keep an accurate account of the churches that support us, you know."

VOLUNTEER: "But he's hollering and screaming in pain, and, calling for you, and..."

MISSIONARY MARVA: "Interruptions, interruptions! It's always something. (Still counting and recording.) Give him an aspirin and tell him to call me in the morning." (Hands her a bottle of aspirins.)

VOLUNTEER: "But, but, he may not last that long! It's really serious, and, and..."

MISSIONARY MARVA: (Puts down book and money, obviously annoyed.)"O.K., O.K. I'm coming. Don't have an aneurysm. It' s just a little snake bite. What a big baby. Can't even stand a little bite." (Continues to mumble as she follows the volunteer out. Scene fades and pans back to St. Peter.)

ST. PETER: "Quite a compassionate little lady, eh, back in the day, as they say."

MISSIONARY MARVA: "Oh, yes. I was always ready to give to others and help, and..."

ST. PETER: "Don't add insult to injury! GUARDS!"

MISSIONARY MARVA: (As guards drag her off protesting.) "But what about all those good deeds? What about all those years of service?!!"

ST. PETER: (Calling after her.) "Yes, but you only served yourself.

(Mumbles to no one in particular.) I just don't get it. I can't understand how people do their own thing, ignore the Bible's teachings, and expect to stroll right on into heaven." (Scratches his head; sits in the big seat.)

—Music. Lights fade and pan in on singer—

Act II
SCENE: II

(Singer and Mime come out)

"DID YOU DO YOUR OWN THING?"
Did you do your own thing, or did you follow God?
Did you do your own thing, or were you just too proud?
God is always, right there to help you Deliver and care
for you too
But if you scorn Him and turn your back on Him You will be
destined to fail

CHORUS:
Just hold your head high, look to the sky,
Tell Him you'll follow Him
Forget your own thing, and tell Him you'll sing,
His praises forever more

Did you do your own thing, or did you heed the Word. Did
you do your own thing, or say you' d never heard, Of all of
God's goodness, to you and to me
He will deliver and care you will see
But if you scorn Him and turn your back on Him
You will be destined to fail.

CHORUS:
Just hold your head high, look to the sky,
Tell Him you'll follow Him
Forget your own thing, and tell Him you'll sing,
His praises forever more
HIS PRAISES FOR-EVER MORE!!!

Did You Do Your Own Thing?

By Betty C. I. McDaniel

Own Thing
Page 1

Own Thing
Page 2

Own Thing
Page 3

Own Thing
Page 4

SCENE III

(Pans back to St. Peter who comments on the words of the song, shakes his head.)

ST. PETER: "NEXT!"

(Very tattered and tom dressed man comes in. Humbly gives paper with his name on it to St. Peter.)

ST. PETER: (Looking at paper.) "Tom... Tettlebomb. Hmmm... Looks like you lead a pretty rough life. Were you one of those street people who slept on vents in the big city, trying to keep warm? Never could get a job, just took the easy way out?"

TOM: "Well, not exactly, sir..."

ST. PETER: (A little irritated) "Let's just run the tape — it's been a long day." "ROLL THE TAPE!"

—-Drums, lights flashing, smoke, etc.—-

(Pans to a street scene. Two or three bums are panhandling; others are laying on vents, digging in trash cans, drinking out of brown bags, etc. Tom enters and begins to give them money and tracks, and whispers words of encouragement. Tells them Jesus loves them, etc.)

TOM: "Here friend. (Gives him money and track.) Remember, God loves you.

Keep the faith." (Repeats the same to a few other bums. Tarries with the last bum.) "Friend, have you heard of the Four Spiritual Laws?" (Bum shakes his head no.) "Well I have good news for you today." (Opens Bible and shares salvation scriptures from Romans: 3:10; 3:23; 6:23; 10:9; 10;13, etc., loud enough so audience can hear.)

Just as he finishes the sinner's prayer with the man...

—Police sirens blare, horns honk—

—All on street scatter except Tom—

POLICEMAN: "All right, Tom. Let's move along. We know you've been giving those old bums your money. Why don't you go back to your suburban home and give your money to charity and leave these streets to us! One day you're going to get hurt!"

TOM: "Thank you, sir. But I prefer doing it my way." (Walks off set right, policeman exits left.)

—Drums, flashing lights, etc.—

(Pan back to St. Peter.)

ST. PETER: "Very impressive. Very good. But is your name in the book? (Thumps it several times.) Let's just take a look. Tom B..., Tom L..., Tom R..., Tom S..., Tom Telly..., Tom Tenny..., TOM TETTLEBOM!! Mercy me! It's there! (Thumps book again, as Tom smiles.) You did it! You made it into heaven!!!" (Shakes his hand.)

—Drum rolls; Loud Music; Praise Team comes out shouting; Gives Tom his long white robe; Crowns him with the "Soul Winners Crown"; Escorts him out into heaven.

ST. PETER: (Looking after Tom, waves, etc.)

Very good. Very good. Now let' s see. (Checks a list.) One more to go and I'm finished for the day. Yippee! I hope this last one is quick and easy —- with NO complications. It's been a long... day, and I do mean LONG! (Yawns and stretches.) NEXT!"

SCENE IV

(Older man runs in and hands St. Peter his name slip and says proudly..._

OLDER MAN: "I'm going to heaven on my momma's prayers."

(St. Peter looks distraught and rolls his eyes upward, but before he can respond, another younger man enters.

YOUNGER MAN: "I'm going to heaven on my poppa's prayers. (Smiles broadly and hands St. Peter his name slip; and leans on his father.)

ST. PETER: (Looking pained and shakes his head, etc.) "And I dared to hope for an EASY and UNCOMPLICATED ending! All right fellas. I'm not even going to try to break it down. I'm too whipped. I'm going to let you listen to these words and see if you can get it. O.K.?" (They nod.)

(Rapper enters)

—Lights fade——Pan in on rapper-

"GIVE IT UP TO THE LORD"

You can't get to heaven on your Momma' s prayers
Not even on your Poppa's or the Saints if you dare
Going to heaven is a single thing
Solo all the way if you want those wings
Wings to fly all over God's heaven
Eating that bread and all that good leaven
Tasting the good things in the great above
Filled with the Holy Ghost and all that love
Smiling and greeting your old friends and kin
Thanking the Lord, you too made it in

CHORUS:
Give it up...to the Lord
Give it up...to the Lord
things will get betta, if you will letta
Jesus in your heart and into your life
Out goes the pain and the heartache and strife
Give it up...to the Lord
Give it up...to the Lord

But how do you get there? You might ask
By following the Word, no easy task
Not in your own strength you surely won't last
But by taking your burdens and woes and cast
Them at the feet of the Savior, Dear
And ask Him to forgive you, and always stay near
(Back to Chorus)

That is the way, give it all up to God
Tell Him you're sorry, for all sin you allowed
To come in your life, when you were so proud You partied
and played that music real loud
But now you know it was to no avail
You felt like a loser and someone who failed
But that was then, and this is now
Thank God almighty He showed you how
(Back to Chorus)

(Pans back to St. Peter)

ST. PETER: "Now do you get it? You have to give it up to the Lord on your own.

You have to accept Jesus Christ for yourself, not through someone else. Did you two ever do that?"

OLDER MAN/YOUNGERMAN: (Nodding together.) Yes sir!!

ST. PETER: (Tiredly) "All right. Let' s take a look. Now what are your names again?

OLDER MAN: "I'm Big Joe Jackson, Sr."

YOUNGER MAN: "I'm Little Joe Jackson, Jr."

ST. PETER: "Is the ' big' and 'little' necessary? Never mind. Let's see... Jackson, Jackson, B., Jackson, C., Jackson, F., Jackson, H., Jackson, I., Jackson, ...

(Men hold hands in anticipation.)

—Jackson, Joe, Sr. (He jumps up and down and shouts!) ...and

—Jackson, Joe, Jr. (He jumps up and down and shouts!)

—and... and... JACKSON, JOE, III!!! (They both stop).

Who's he...?"

OLDER MAN: "It ain' t mine!". (Looks at younger.)

YOUNGER MAN: "It ain't mine!" (Both begin to squabble.)

ST. PETER: "Gentlemen! Gentlemen! Let's not lose sight of the bigger picture. Whoever Joe Jackson the III is... he has to make it in on his own too. Right? (Both grin and· nod.)

The good news is that you BOTH made it in! WELCOME TO HEAVEN!!!"

—They begin to shout! Praise Team comes in—

—Music plays, Drum rolls—

—Praise Team robes them, etc.—-

GRAND FINALE: All the saved come back on stage and join with the others singing "There's a Crown Waiting for You". The unsaved try to sneak in and are caught by the guards who haul them off the stage. All are singing and dancing. Verses are sung with much swaying, hands raised, and at a joyful gait. The Final Chorus is done with much precision and choreography and creativity to add to the Play's final moments!

"THERE'S A CROWN WAITING FOR YOU"

There's a crown, waiting in glory, for you and for me
There's a crown, waiting in glory, for you and for me
If you've done all that you can, and you' ve helped your
fellow man
Then there's a crown (There' s a crown)
Waiting in glory (Waiting in glory)
Just for you (There's a crown waiting for you...)
Did you take Him in your heart, from His Word you
did not part
Then there's a crown (There's a crown)
Waiting in glory (Waiting in glory)
Just for you (There's a crown waiting for you...)
As you lived in this old land, did you follow God's own plan
Then there's a crown (There's a crown)
Waiting in glory (Waiting in glory)
Just for you (There' s a crown waiting for you...)

Chorus:
On that great and crowning day
Jesus shall wipe your tears away
He will say you passed the test
Come on home and take your rest
I've a crown, I've a robe
I have riches all untold
Waiting in heaven (Waiting in heaven)
Just for you (There' s a crown waiting for you...)

There's a Crown Waiting for You

By Betty C. I. McDaniel

Piano

There's a Crown
Page 1

There's a Crown
Page 2

There's a Crown
Page 3

There's a Crown
Page 4

(Everyone exits and leaves St. Peter there alone.)

SCENE: V

(St. Peter yawns and stretches and begins picking up things.)

ST. PETER: "What a LONG... day, and I do mean LONG. It's time for ME to go home and get some rest. (Tries to open the door and finds it locked. He pulls and tugs but to no avail.)

VOICE: "ROLL THE TAPE!"

(St. Peter puts his hands on his hips and frowns.)

VOICE: "Just kidding." (Door now opens.)

ST. PETER: (Grins, opens door, and looks back at the audience.) Bye yawl. See you in heaven."

—Music, Lights, Curtains—

(Curtain Call. All actors may be acknowledged at this time.)

MINISTER: Sums up the play and attests to its humor, but also to its seriousness. **The Call to Salvation** is given at this point. Newly saved are ministered to and encouraged to attend Bible Teaching Churches to grow in their newly found faith.

BENEDICTION

May God Bless you as you minister to God's people through the art of theater.

THE LONG LEATHER BAG

Author: Unknown

Source: Told by my mother, Bettie Mary Isaac

Requested by: My daughter, Linda

Once upon a time, long, long, ago, there was a widow woman who lived in a small shack with her three daughters. They had very little, just a few coins and dollars, left by her deceased husband, that she kept in an old leather bag that she stashed away in the top of her closet. There was a wicked, old witch, peeping in the window, and saw where she kept her life's savings. One night she came in and stole the old leather bag; and ran away and escaped.

When the family got up the next morning, and the mother saw that the bag was gone, she was very distraught. The oldest daughter said she saw the wicked witch hanging around the day before, and she was probably the one who stole it. She told her mother that she would go out and find her and their leather bag of money. Her mother blessed her and sent her on her way.

She started down the road and came upon a sheep. She said to the sheep:

Sheep of mine, sheep of mine

Have you seen a maid of mine?
With a wig, with a wag
With a long leather bag
She stole all the money that we ever had

The sheep said, "Sheer me, sheer me; I haven't been sheered in a long, long time."
The oldest daughter said, "I don't have time to sheer you. I have to find our leather bag!"

She continued down the road a bit; and ran into a cow. She said to the cow:

Cow of mine, cow of mine
Have you seen a maid of mine?
With a wig, with a wag
With a long leather bag
She stole all the money that we ever had

The cow said, "Milk me, milk me; I haven't been milked in a long, long time.

She said, "I don't have time to milk you. I have to find our leather bag.

She continued down the road and came upon an old horse. She said to the horse:

Horse of mine, horse of mine
Have you seen a maid of mine?
With a wig, with a wag
With a long leather bag
She stole all the money that we ever had

The horse said, "Rub me, rub me; I haven't been rubbed in a long, long, time."
The oldest daughter said, "I don't have time to rub you. I have to find our leather bag!"

She continued down the road and ran into a windmill. She said to the windmill"

Mill of mine, Mill of mine
Have you seen a maid of mine?
With a wig, with a wag
With a long leather bag
She stole all the money that we ever had

The windmill said, "Turn me, turn me; I haven't been turned in a long, long time.
She told the windmill that she didn't have time; she had to find the leather bag.

Just then the wicked witch jumped out from behind the windmill, and turned the oldest daughter into a stone, with her wand.

After several days went by and the oldest daughter didn't come home, the second daughter told her mother she would go look for her sister and the leather bag. The mother also gave her a blessing, and she started down the road.

She came upon the sheep and said:

Sheep of mine, sheep of mine
Have you seen a maid of mine?
With a wig, with a wag
With a long leather bag
She stole all the money that we ever had

The sheep said, "Sheer me, sheer me; I haven't been sheered in a long, long time.
The second daughter said, "I don't have time to sheer you. I have to find our leather bag!"

She continued down the road and ran into the cow. She said to the cow:

Cow of mine, cow of mine
Have you seen a maid of mine?
With a wig, with a wag
With a long leather bag
She stole all the money that we ever had
The cow said, "Milk me, milk me; I haven't been milked in a long, long time. She said to the cow, "I don't have time to milk you; I have to find our leather bag!"

The second sister continued down the road and came upon a horse. She said to the horse:

Horse of mine, horse of mine
Have you seen a maid of mine?
With a wig, with a wag
With a long leather bag
She stole all the money that we ever had

The horse said, "Rub me, rub me, I haven't been rubbed in a long, long time."
The sister said, "I don't have time to rub you. I have to find our leather bag!"

She continued down the road until she came upon the windmill.

Mill of mine, Mill of mine
Have you seen a maid of mine?
With a wig, with a wag
With a long leather bag
She stole all the money that we ever had

The Windmill said, "Turn me, turn me; I haven't been turned in a long, long time."
The second daughter said, "I don't have time to turn you; I have to find our leather bag!"

Just then the wicked witch jumped out from behind the windmill, and turned her into a stone, and she lay next to the stone of her older sister.

When the youngest sister saw that her two older sisters weren't returning, she told her mother that she would go and look for them and the leather bag. The mother reluctantly agreed, knowing this was the last daughter that she had. Nevertheless, she blessed her too and sent her on her way.

The youngest daughter started down the road and came across the sheep. She said to the sheep:

Sheep of mine, sheep of mine
Have you seen a maid of mine?
With a wig, with a wag
With a long leather bag
She stole all the money that we ever had

The sheep said, "Sheer me, sheer me, I haven't been sheered in a long, long time.
The youngest sister picked up some scissors and sheered the sheep. Then the sheep said, "The wicked witch went that-a-way." The youngest daughter thanked him and went on down the road.

She came upon the cow, and asked him:

Cow of mine, cow of mine
Have you seen a maid of mine?
With a wig, with a wag
With a long leather bag
She stole all the money that we ever had

The cow said, "Milk me, milk me, I haven't been milked in a long, long time."
The youngest daughter pulled up the stool and pail; and sat down and milked the cow.
The cow said, "The wicked witch went that-a-way." She thanked him and went on her way.

She continued down the road and ran into an old horse. She said to the horse:

Horse of mine, horse of mine
Have you seen a maid of mine?
With a wig, with a wag
With a long leather bag
She stole all the money that we ever had

The horse said, "Rub me, rub me. I haven't been rubbed in a long, long time."

The horse said, "The wicked witch went that-a-way.

The youngest daughter thanked him and continued down the road and ran into the old windmill. She said:

Mill of mine, mill of mine
Have you seen a maid of mine?
With a wig, with a wag
With a long leather bag
She stole all the money that we ever had

The windmill said, "Turn me, turn me; I haven't been turned in a long, long time."

The little girl turned and turned the windmill. The windmill said, "Hide inside of me before the wicked witch comes back. You look tired. Rest your head on those two little stones over there and take a nap. The little girl did.

A little while later, the wicked witch came back and yelled at the windmill saying, "Where is that third daughter? I know she's here somewhere. There were three of them."

The windmill said, "Come a little closer; I can't hear you." The witch repeated what she had said, and the windmill kept urging her to come closer, and closer, because he couldn't hear her. When she came really close, he whirled his blades around real fast, and caught her up in them, and flung her high into the air to her death.

He called the youngest daughter out, and told her to pick up the witch's wand, and touch the two stones that were before her. When she did so, her two sisters re-appeared, and they hugged and cried and had a great reunion. The windmill told them where to find the old leather bag. They thanked the windmill, found their leather bag, and ran all the way home to momma, and they lived happily ever after. The End.

CPSIA information can be obtained
at www.ICGtesting.com
Printed in the USA
BVHW052311240721
612674BV00003B/6